How the small "a" (autism) taught me to PRAY BIG

Being thankful to GOD
in the midst of your greatest test,
in order to have your...<u>Testimony</u>!

M.J. Wotany

gatekeeper press
Where Authors are Family
Columbus, Ohio

How the small "a" (autism) taught me to PRAY BIG

Published by Gatekeeper Press
2167 Stringtown Rd, Suite 109
Columbus, OH 43123-2989
www.GatekeeperPress.com

ISBN (hardcover): 9781642376005
ISBN (paperback): 9781642375992
eISBN: 9781642375985

Printed in the United States of America

How the small "a" (autism) taught me to
PRAY
BIG

"Always stand on God's promises"

—Best wishes

Nightes

4/24/19

Contents

My Purpose

THIS GUIDE IS intended for parents with children recently diagnosed with ASD (Autism Spectrum Disorder) or who are already going through this journey and have been dealing with the difficulties that come with this journey.

My overall goal is to shed some light on how to reduce the burden placed upon us once we receive the diagnosis by combining all that I have learned throughout this process and making it easier for others. Rather than going from one website to another or one book to another for early interventions and ideas on how to help your kiddo, I wanted to put together a reference guide about our journey, from where we started and what options we had to how we went about obtaining resources.

After discussing our journey when our son was diagnosed with ASD, I'll talk about how we maneuvered through ALL the stages of coping. Throughout the chapters, I discuss the different coping strategies and how we moved forward from denial to anger, to bargaining, to depression, and ultimately ended up at the acceptance stage where we got the help we needed for our kiddo.

Longtime missionary Jackie Pullinger once stated that "God wants us to have soft hearts and hard feet. The trouble with so many of us is that we have hard hearts and soft feet." My ultimate aspiration is that you will allow me to walk with you during this journey. I realized during this journey that in order to make a difference in the lives of others in this world, I will need hard feet as I travel along tough paths and face the challenges before me.

Lastly, early intervention strategies and additional resources are mentioned to help you throughout the rest of this journey. Throughout this book, I try to walk with you each step of the way so that we can grow together and spiritually empower ourselves!

"Three things will last forever—faith, hope and love—
and the greatest of these is love."
—1 Corinthians 13:13

"No one is useless in this world
who lightens the burdens of another."
—Charles Dickens

Acknowledgements

FIRST AND FOREMOST I would like to give all honor and glory to our Lord and Savior Jesus Christ who without Him in my life none of this would be possible. I thank GOD for giving me the privilege to share His Word with others in order to worship, magnify and glorify His name. I truly believe that God uses our trials and tribulations as a testimony to His power and might. Even in our valleys we must maintain our faith, thank Him for His tender mercies and grace that are renewed everyday and put all out trusts in Him.

I would like to thank my parents, Dr. Joseph and Mrs. Emma for establishing the foundation of faith in me so early in my childhood; my siblings, John, Mary and Elsie for their continued encouragement and accountability as we each walk through the journey of faith. My parents taught me that God will always be there in my darkest moments, He will give me wisdom when I ask for it and cover me under his mighty wings whenever I call His name.

I would also I like to thank Jayson's team of healthcare professionals who have been with us through this journey and continue to be with us. I want to thank you all for your time, your dedication and all which you have poured into Jayson that has gotten him this far. Each and everyone one of you holds a special place in my heart. Special thanks to Mrs. Basore (the best teacher ever) and her team, Ms. Marisa, Mrs. Lisa, Ms. Megan,

Ms. Sharon, Ms. Fatima, Ms. Jessie and last but definitely not least Ms. Madison! You have been with us the longest. Thank you so much for never giving up on Jayson. Thank you for staying with us, even when you didn't have to. Thank you for pushing him, being so strict with him and loving him. From the bottom of my heart, I appreciate all you have done for us and I truly consider you as part of our family.

Lastly, I will not mention these two names, however they know who they are and the influence they have made in my life. To my special prayer partner, if it wasn't for you, I don't know where I would be, mentality, spiritually, physically and emotionally. You have supported me in more ways than I can count. Thank you for your advice, your encouraging words and especially the time you took to teach me the Word of God. Thank you for believing in me when I didn't believe in myself. Thank you for teaching me about the importance of prayer, why it's imperative to live life kneeling down daily, with our arms pointing up to the sky and even more prevalent, teaching me that the Christ of miracles then, is the same Christ of miracles today. I truly thank you my personal person! Now to that other person, you know who you are! Since you don't want me to acknowledge you, all I will say is - thank you so much for always being there for me, supporting me and being my other half!

An extra special thanks to my husband and children - you all are the best of the best! I especially want to thank Jayson for his resilience and strength since we started this journey together in 2014. You have taught me how to be patient, depend on God's strength, but more importantly, because of you, I grew in my relationship and faith in Jesus Christ. You continue to amaze me and I can't wait to see the day you give your testimony on stage in front of a group of people, exalting the name of our Lord even more! We are indeed blessed! Thank you Lord!

Prologue

"We steward the only message on planet earth that can give people what their hearts need most, which is hope. Hope that sins can be forgiven. Hope that prayers can be answered. Hope that doors of opportunity, that seemed locked, can be opened. Hope that broken relationships can be reconciled. Hope that diseased bodies can be healed. Hope that damaged trust can be restored. Hope that dead churches can be resurrected . . . Of all people, we must claim that hope and live in it and radiate it to others. And we must proclaim that message of hope to everyone God gives us the opportunity to influence"

—Bill Hybels

THIS REFERENCE GUIDE is written first of all to give GOD all the glory and praise for the many things he has done in my life, but most importantly for giving me the biggest test and blessing me with an autistic child who taught me about the power **with, in,** and **of** prayer. I pray that this book makes a great impact, not only on your child, but also on you as a caregiver. I would like to address the difficulties that foreigners living in the United States face as it relates to their children being diagnosed with autism. I hope my story provides you with insight on how to tackle the difficulties associated with this diagnosis and how to come out on the other side praising, worshiping, and thanking GOD for giving you this test which will turn into your greatest testimony in your life in the mighty name of Jesus!

Secondly, I always tease my family, friends, colleagues, and associates that we all have some level of autism, but some of us just manage it in different ways . . . please laugh. According to the Autism Speaks website, "Autism, or autism spectrum disorder (ASD), refers to a broad range of conditions characterized by challenges with social skills, repetitive behaviors, speech, and nonverbal communication." If one looks really closely at this definition, we can say that we "normal" individuals, who have not been diagnosed with autism, can at times have difficulties communicating and interacting socially, depending on the environment we find ourselves in. We, too, can be on the spectrum if we have these difficulties that we have not yet addressed. However, my purpose is not to over-examine what autism is, but rather to suggest what you can do after getting the diagnosis from a healthcare provider who specializes in early childhood development. My goal is to empower you and to give you resources that can enable you and your child to institute early intervention strategies to help stop the progression and further delay in those above-mentioned areas of difficulties, with the ultimate goal of making ALL OUR KIDDOS SELF-SUFFICIENT!

Thirdly, autism doesn't define who you are, who your child is, or how they will be in the future. However, we must empower ourselves and other parents. Everyone must do their research and do what is best for their kiddo. As parents, we must be our children's most ardent advocates—not the school, or the psychiatrist, or the social worker, or the daycare provider—or anyone else you ask to help your child in this process. It's us, the parents, who must assume this responsibility because we ultimately have the best solutions and because we know our kiddos intimately, in ways these outside resources do NOT. Later, as you read our story, you will realize that I was not only limiting my way of thinking, but also limiting my child and, most importantly, GOD when all of this started in 2014. But as I studied the Bible, I saw that perfection, the beauty of the LORD we serve, and because HE is the vine and we are the branches and also heirs to HIS throne, we, too, are perfect! It is wise to remember that when given a problem, you will either take that problem and make it bigger or take it and make it smaller. Our approach to our problems makes the biggest difference, and in this instance for me, inviting GOD to take control of my child and his difficulties was the best decision I ever made.

"For ever since the world was created, people have seen the earth and sky. Through everything God made, they can clearly see His invisible qualities—His eternal power and divine nature. So they have no excuse for not knowing God."

—Romans 1:20

Let's dive in!

Growing Up

"In the beginning the Word already existed. The Word was with God, and the Word was God. He existed in the beginning with God. God created everything through him, and nothing was created except through him. The Word gave life to everything that was created, and his life brought light to everyone. The light shines in the darkness, and the darkness can never extinguish it."

—John 1:1-5

Just as everyone's story is unique and different, so is mine. My family is originally from Cameroon, West Africa and moved to the United States in June 1990. My dad was offered a job teaching French in Kansas City, Missouri, where we spent over thirteen years of our lives. We later relocated to Salisbury, Maryland, because he was offered a job as a high school principal. My family and I grew up as Catholic(s). Living in my parents' house meant that we had to go to mass every Sunday. I grew up in a family with one brother and two sisters—I was child number three. During moments as children, into our youth, and later into our adult lives, we each started making our own decisions about which denominations we wanted to be a part of. I remember that our parents always taught us about the importance of going to church but not really about the importance of having a RELATIONSHIP with GOD.

In 1995, my older sister visited a non-Catholic church and came back and told my younger sister and me about it. She came home with such excitement after visiting that church and told us that she found a church that she loved and that they read the Bible there. We were like, "What? Tell us more!" She wanted to continue going, though our dad never wanted to hear of it. This created a big rift in the house, but she continued to go to the church secretly because she didn't want to get in trouble and because she was on fire for GOD. In 1996, before she went away to college, she gave each us a Bible and told us to read it in order to have a relationship with GOD. As the years went by, we read it, but we didn't really understand what we were reading.

More than twenty years have passed, and here we are, all grown up, married, and living separate lives. I met my husband in Germany in April 2007. By 2009, we were happily married in Denmark. We eventually settled in United States in 2011 when his documents were approved by the government. In 2012, we had our first child, Emmanuella, who was a great bundle of joy. She had some speech difficulties early on, but with the help of a program called Infants and Toddlers, she was able to overcome this obstacle. During this time, I would say that my relationship with God existed but was not consistent. I knew HE was there, but I felt like I could handle everything on my own and would only call on HIM if things got really bad. But how many of you know that there are bad things in the world that we don't see with our physical eyes? There are evil forces always fighting to make sure we don't succeed, and let's not forget what the purpose of the thief is—to steal and kill and destroy (John 10:10). We will later discuss ways to build your relationship with GOD in order to be empowered by the Holy Spirit.

"The Lord formed me from the beginning, before He created anything else."

—*Proverbs 8:22*

Our Story . . . Pathway to ASD

"Prepare your shields, and advance into battle!"

—Jeremiah 46:3

O UR JOURNEY STARTED in May 2014 when my husband fell sick and was hospitalized. His illness came as a complete shock to us, considering that he was perfectly healthy prior to his illness. At first, all we knew was that his illness was defined as seizure-like activity. After arriving at the hospital, they did blood-work, a CT scan, and an MRI of his brain, but we were still waiting for answers.

Worst of all, I was six months pregnant with our son. That time in our lives was the most difficult time, I think, in our relationship and in our family. At the time of my husband's illness, Emmanuella was two years old. She witnessed her father in distress, a scene I will never get out of my head. In the early stages of his illness, he couldn't remember his name, where he was, where he was born, or who I was. Nothing made any sense to him. I was so afraid for him that I didn't have the time to think of myself and the fact that I was pregnant. He was admitted to the intensive care unit for what felt like an eternity. With the uncertainty of his illness, the extended hours in the hospital, and my work schedule, we decided to send our daughter out of state to my older sister's place.

After several months of my husband being in and out of the hospital, balancing my job schedule, and taking care of him, I was really stressed and overwhelmed. This season in our lives not only took a physical toll on us, but an emotional toll as well. There were times during his hospitalization that my faith in God was nonexistent. I saw this man in front of me, day in and day out, slowly deteriorating, and I couldn't even pray. My thought process was, 'Oh well, even if I pray, God will still do what He wants to.' The best I could do was to ask God to have HIS will be done.

I remember spending nights at the hospital sleeping on a chair or on a hard side bar they called a bed. There were times during his hospitalization that my husband would refuse parts of the treatment plan. I would get so angry with him, thinking, 'These are doctors! This is what they do ALL day long! How can he refuse their recommendations?' Now, in the present, I can appreciate the fact that he was being guided by the Holy Spirit. The doctors were able to do a full workup to determine if it was a stroke, and they later diagnosed him with severe cluster migraines, which haven't occurred again since.

One thing I haven't mentioned is that the morning of my husband falling sick, I remember so vividly talking to GOD and just asking him to change things in my husband's life. Though I didn't have a relationship with GOD, I considered myself a kind and caring individual. I tried my best to build and maintain healthy relationships with others and tried not to hurt them, and if I did, I did my best to quickly apologize. However, in the weeks and months leading up to my husband's illness, he got into several arguments with my family members and his; he was also so angry, bitter, full of resentment, and just plain mean. I was getting so frustrated by the way he was treating others that I didn't know what else to do. So that morning while I was putting laundry in the machine (I remember this like it was yesterday!), I was asking GOD to just do something to SHAKE and WAKE my husband, and a few hours later, it happened! And I thank GOD for this testimony in my husband's life today.

After a prolonged recovery period and putting all our minds and hearts into prayers, it changed our mindset about who GOD was. Though I had rededicated my life to Christ several years prior, I was not necessarily living a "Christian life." Don't get me wrong, I wasn't doing crazy things, but I also wasn't making time to get to know who GOD was and reading HIS WORD. I rarely touched my Bible, and things were okay in life.

May, June, and July went by, and August eventually came. I guess the stress from my husband's situation really caused my body a lot of pain that I never realized until later when I sat down and started thinking back on things. Not only did I have the usual pregnancy pains, I also had a pinched nerve on the right side of my back which was caused by days of sleeping on those so-called hospital visitor "beds." I had completely shut out the fact that I was pregnant. The only two things I did consistently during the pregnancy were taking my prenatal vitamins and attending my doctor appointments. At thirty-two weeks pregnant, the baby was still in a breech position. The doctors assured me that he would turn as the pregnancy continued. Unfortunately, that did not happen. But in all things, GOD was faithful through the process. With all that we had gone through, we both knew that we had to name this child something really special. The healing we received from GOD in the process of all of this could only be described as a miracle. We decided on the name Jayson, which in Hebrew means TO HEAL!

"There your enemies shouted their victorious battle cries; there they set up their battle standards."

—*Psalm 74:4*

Notes

The Journey of
ASD Begins

"Then they said, 'Ask God whether or not our journey will be successful.'"

—Judges 18:5

URING OUR PRENATAL visits to the doctor, we were originally told that our due date was July 26, but we all know that babies come when they want. We waited and waited, and on August 6 at 12:54 a.m., we had our beautiful, 8-pound 7-ounce baby boy. He came out with his eyes wide open and was so strong and ready to conquer the world. It was as though his eyes didn't need time to adjust to light like other kids usually need because he was already living in the "light." He just didn't look ordinary to us. He came out looking like he had seen a lot during his time in the womb and was already ready to face the world. This is Jayson at six months of age.

Jayson was really a blessing to us. He slept really well during the night and had no eating problems. The most difficult thing we struggled with throughout his infancy, into his second and third years, was his eczema. Thankfully, my brother referred me to company called MEM's (highly recommend!), that make their own shea butter lotion from scratch, and we haven't had any problems since. Jayson grew extremely well and we had no complaints. The primary care doctor, however, told us to be mindful that he might be a big kid and to watch of his intake of juice and milk as he got to one year of age. To us, it was okay, being that we had heard horror stories of kids who struggled with eating and also remembering that Emmanuella had struggled a little with feeding when she was about eighteen months to two years of age.

More pics of our bundle of joy!

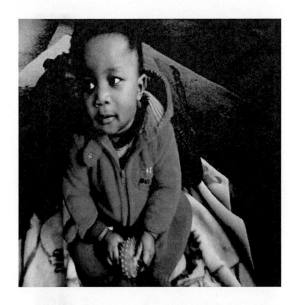

By nine months, Jayson was already going up and down the steps, walking extremely well, and getting into any and everything. I remember that it was nine months just because it took almost one year before his older sister could walk.

Now here comes what we will call our "trials in life." By one year of age, Jayson was still not saying any words, no *mama* or *dada*, nothing. After going to his wellness visit, the primary care doctor stated that she really didn't have any concerns and just mentioned that some kids are late talkers, primarily boys. So we left it alone. Fast-forward a bit, and by eighteen months, he started saying a few words—primarily things he saw on TV like "Dora" and "backpack." He was saying them clearly; however, still no *mama* or *dada*. We still didn't have any concerns and just thought to ourselves that our child would talk when he was ready.

By the time Jayson turned two, his speech declined, and he quickly stopped talking or repeating what he knew. The only repeated behaviors that we noticed were that he liked to jump a lot, to spin in circles while looking out of the corner of his eye, and to line things up. He also kept seeking pressure by hitting his chin and forehead on hard surfaces or on other people's firm body parts, etc. By now, the pediatrician was getting a little worried and said she didn't understand what was happening. She suggested that we have Infants and Toddlers come to our home. The primary care doctor also ordered a hearing test to be done with sedation, since Jayson was such a tough patient and never wanted anyone to look at him, let alone touch him. An auditory brainstem response (ABR) test was completed at one of our local hospitals. Thankfully, the staff was patient with us, and we were able to get one ear done before he woke up from the anesthesia. Though they were only able to complete testing on one ear, they concluded that Jayson had no issues with his hearing and that his speech difficulties were not due to any hearing loss or difficulties.

For those who don't know what Infants and Toddlers is, it's a Baltimore County program that allows children who have either minimal or significant developmental delays in speech or occupational therapy to receive home services specific to that delay. After they evaluated us, they decided to have a special education teacher come weekly to help with Jayson's speech delays.

Unfortunately, our first teacher was extremely young and inexperienced. To make matters even worse, she was pregnant and would soon be going on maternity leave. At that time, though I understood the importance of women having time with their families, I was also 1) kind of selfish and wanted someone who knew what they were doing, and 2) wanting and needing consistency because they were coming into our home and my child needed help.

As time progressed, I really could see the severity and how behind Jayson was in speaking and behavior. Nonetheless, the special education teacher went on maternity leave and that left us without any services. The agency put us on hold while looking for another teacher or the "right" teacher who could better serve Jayson's needs. After waiting for over three months for services, we were finally able to get an autism specialty teacher—though Jayson was not yet officially diagnosed. The autism specialty teacher was really good and patient with Jayson. I first met her at an outdoor summer group where she was teaching younger kids dance. She was playing with bubbles and just had a lot of energy within her. When I learned that she would become our child's teacher, I was ecstatic. When she started coming to our home, we began to see a lot of changes. She gave me a lot to read about ASD and wanted me to try to understand what might be going on with Jayson. After each of Jayson's sessions, we would discuss what I read the week prior. She even found the time to answer my questions. I appreciated not only the work she was doing with Jayson, but the time she took to sit down and discuss with me what seemed at that time such a confusing prospect of a possible diagnosis. This really allowed me to know more about what I was facing, and though Jayson wasn't officially diagnosed yet, I felt that she was already "labeling" him. In the literature she gave me, I could see that Jayson had some of the behaviors and speech characteristics that were consistent with autism.

Phase 1) DENIAL started to pop into my head around this time. In addition to the reading materials, Ms. Jillian gave me a long list of things to do and people to call. On the "to call" list was Kennedy Krieger Institute, a world-renowned organization located in Baltimore that provides inpatient and outpatient services to children and adolescents with learning disabilities and disorders of the brain, spinal cord, and musculoskeletal system. Before the end of that home visit, I called Kennedy Krieger to schedule our evaluation. We were placed on a six-month waiting list. Six months may feel like an eternity, but remember that this organization is known nationwide for their expertise in child and adolescent development. We had no choice but to wait.

As a side note, I would love to encourage those of you outside the state of Maryland to make an effort to schedule an appointment with Kennedy Krieger Institute. Trust me, it is definitely worth the trip. I was just happy an institution like Kennedy Krieger was not only in my state but in the next county. I was happy to be placed on the waiting list because I knew that getting Jayson into Kennedy Krieger would pay off in the future.

We continued to have weekly services with the special education teacher, focusing on Jayson's speech. She also recommended that an evaluation be done for occupational therapy to work on gross motor skills, sensory issues, dressing, feeding, etc. The evaluation was completed and occupational therapy started. The occupational therapist started addressing Jayson's sensory difficulties and then worked on his physical and motor skills. In addition, Jayson started a three-day-a-week classroom interaction program with three of his peers called Connections. Connections is also administered through the Infants and Toddlers program, and it is designed in preparation for school once a child turns three years old.

During this time, since Jayson wasn't making much progress, the special education teacher suggested that we have their psychiatrist come to our home to evaluate Jayson for autism so that we would know how to proceed further. The psychiatric evaluation was completed a month later, and after a week or so, the psychiatrist came back with the report that Jayson was, in fact, autistic, but on the mild side of the spectrum. This was definitely when the denial phase really started.

Though I was getting Jayson the help he needed, I still saw what he was going through as a DELAY, not a diagnosis. I just thought to myself, 'Oh, he will be like my daughter who had a delay in speech, but after a few sessions he will be fine.' But I knew that by age two, my daughter was at least saying a few things and responding to things and people, while Jayson was not doing that in any way, shape, or form. Family and friends continued to encourage me by saying that boys are naturally late at doing certain things, especially speaking, and that Jayson would be fine. They, too, aided in my denial phase, though I know they were being supportive in their own way.

Denial is typical in any situation in life, but I don't want you to spend too much time in this phase. There are so many interventions that can be done after the diagnosis, and time is of the essence! But I also don't want to rush you. I know that there is a lot going through your mind right now, but I promise you, it does get better as you move through each day.

To move forward:

- Cry, cry, and cry . . . then take deep breaths!
- Remind yourself that it is going to be okay.
- Remind yourself that it is not about you—it's about your kiddo.
- Wipe your eyes, look in the mirror, and say, "It's going to be alright."
- Make the necessary phone calls to start the early intervention process!
- Keep in mind that even though you are dealing with denial, you don't want to hinder your kiddo's progress in getting the help they need!

Before I move on to Phase 2 (Anger), I would like to address the spectrum a little more. Without going into too much detail about how Jayson's results were assessed, below is a chart provided by the Centers for Disease Control and Prevention (CDC) on how to explore and/or explain the level at which an individual can fall on the spectrum, which will depend on their level at either the left or the right. These symptoms may vary widely from person to person.

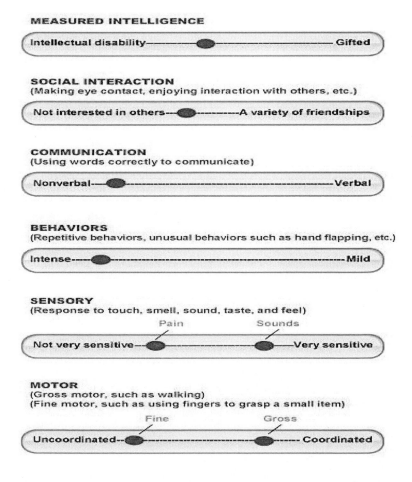

Because Jayson was so young, the psychiatrist focused on all categories except intelligence. After hearing the results, a lot of emotions were going on in our household because 1) no one wants to hear that their child is having this difficulty and that they can't fix them, and 2) in our culture, where people are not that well informed about what autism is, it was really hard for my husband to understand what was happening.

Notes

Phase 2) ANGER begins! My husband kept saying, "Jayson will speak when he will speak," and I was thinking, 'There is nothing wrong with that, but in the meantime, we might as well get all the additional support we can, while we wait for him to start talking.' This is where a lot of foreigners go wrong. Just because you are getting help for your child, it doesn't mean that you are "accepting" anything! Let me say this again. *Just because you are getting help for your child, it doesn't mean that you are "accepting" anything!* At a certain point in our household, Jayson's diagnosis put a huge strain on our marriage, and I felt like I was the one doing everything. I was the one doing all the appointments and the running around. Anger started to be a huge part of this journey for me. I know you companions will understand this a lot, but anger easily creeps in, especially if 1) you and your partner are not on the same page or supporting one another, and 2) you are struggling to understand why this is happening to your child, an innocent child at that.

This was the point in my life that I felt the loneliest, though I was married. Imagine, we just got this diagnosis and instead of it bringing us together, it separated us. I was really angry at my husband, at the world, and at myself. I was questioning GOD a lot, like, 'Why me? Why now? What did I do?' What kept me going, let me be honest, was the fact that GOD gave me the strength and that I was doing everything I could for my son. This is the reason why it is so important when we speak of laying down the right foundation for your children, because during this part of my life, I nearly crumbled. But Jayson was my child, and I was not going to let him fail, no matter what happened to me.

To move forward to the next phase:

- Encourage yourself (don't keep it bottled up).
- Talk to others about your pain and frustrations—your church group or whoever is in your support network (you need them most during this phase).
- See a therapist if needed.
- Lean on support from outsiders if necessary (at times, only those who have gone through what you are going through truly understand what is happening!).
- Continue to put services in place for your kiddo.
- Don't let denial and anger stop you from moving forward and getting the services your kiddo needs to start making progress!

Six months finally passed, and the journey to Kennedy Krieger started. The experience was a two-day process that lasted about six or seven hours each day. At the end of day two, families meet with a social worker to discuss available services. Thankfully, the social worker we were assigned to was exceptional and gave us so many resources that I wasn't even aware of. My companions, the minute someone is able to empower you, you should take that empowerment and run with it (I mean it . . . RUN with it), and that's how we felt after leaving Kennedy Krieger Institute that day. They educated us about additional services, such as outpatient speech therapy, occupational therapy, respite services, ABA (applied behavioral analysis) services, early achievements through Kennedy Krieger – even how to obtain free diapers and pull-ups.

Since Jayson had spent a significant amount of time (in my opinion) with Infants and Toddlers and the Connections program, I was hoping to see some improvement, but nothing was happening. He was still having difficulties expressing himself, and speech was still hard for him. Playing and interacting with his peers was really tough for him, and though I hoped my GOD would work everything out for our good, I didn't know what else to do. My thinking started to shift, and I began to look at myself as the possible cause of the problem. This was when I reached the next phase:

Notes

Phase 3) BARGAINING started. I started thinking to myself that if I hadn't slept at the hospital when my husband was sick and put my body through so much, maybe Jayson wouldn't have this problem. I thought, 'If only I had taken better care of myself while taking care of my husband, this wouldn't be happening. Or maybe it was the type of formula I fed him when he was a baby.' I mean, my companions, a lot came to my head during this phase. I wondered if maybe, just maybe, I had done something differently, Jayson would not be going through all of this.

But honestly, this is another phase that I don't want you to be in for long. It is another setback, and we don't need setbacks during this journey of ours! As Joel Osteen states:

> See, when you drive home today, you've got a big windshield on the front of your car. And you've got a little bitty rearview mirror. And the reason the windshield is so large and the rearview mirror is so small is because what's happened in your past is not near as important as what is in your future.

Let's try to move forward and see what we can do about the future for our kiddos, though I truly understand that it's not easy.

To move forward to the next phase:

- Cry a little more and wipe your eyes.
- Let go of the past.
- Look to the future.
- Acknowledge and accept that there wasn't anything you did wrong. Keep repeating this to yourself until it sinks in!
- Follow up on your early intervention services.

- Continue to get the support you need to feel balanced (mentally, emotionally, physically, psychologically, spiritually, etc.).

- Continue to see a therapist if needed.

- Though you might still be experiencing denial, anger, and bargaining, please continue to get the additional services your kiddo needs to learn and make progress.

As Jayson's journey was continuing and he was getting closer to three years old, Infants and Toddlers gave us the option of either discharging him from their program or beginning a classroom IEP (Individualized Education Program) or continuing with them and the same home services they had been providing. I will discuss later how we made our decision for an IEP.

Before the end of our appointment with the social worker on day two at Kennedy Krieger, I completed the referral paperwork for the Early Achievements Program. This is a program at Kennedy Krieger that allows your child to be in a classroom with three to five other students, being supervised by a speech pathologist and one or two therapeutic assistants. We were later notified that Jayson was admitted into this program, which has a long waiting list. And as I mentioned earlier, since Jayson wasn't making much progress, we decided to remove him from the Connections program and accept his spot at Kennedy Krieger. If something is not working for you and your kiddo, don't accept it. This only means you are wasting valuable time, time during which you can put your kiddo in something else that they can benefit from. At this time, I also began researching which Applied Behavior Analysis (ABA) company we could use that would take our insurance. Everything was happening so fast and all at the same time. Below is what Jayson's schedule looked like in July, August, and September 2017.

M.J. Wotany

July 2017

Sunday	Monday	Tuesday	Wednesday	Thursday	Friday	Saturday
						1
2	3	4	5 ✓ Early Achievements 9am	6 ✓ Early Achievements 9am	7	8
9	10 ✓ Early Achievements 9am ✓ Jays IEP meeting 1pm	11 ✓ Early Achievements 9am ✓ Ms. Sue 12pm	12 ✓ Early Achievements 9am	13 ✓ Early Achievements 9am ✓ Dr. Simon 12:20pm ✓ Ms. Jillian 12pm	14	15
16	17 ✓ Early Achievements 9am	18 ✓ Early Achievements 9am ✓ Ms. Sue 12pm	19 ✓ Early Achievements 9am ✓ Ms. Sue 12pm	20 ✓ Early Achievements 9am ✓ Ms. Jillian 12pm	21	22
23	24 ✓ Early Achievements 9am ✓ Ms. Megan 12:30pm	25 ✓ Early Achievements 9am	26 ✓ Early Achievements 9am ✓ Ms. Jillian 12pm	27 ✓ Early Achievements 9am	28 ✓ ABA 1pm	29
30	31 ✓ Early Achievements 9am					

August 2017

Title

Subtitle

Sunday	Monday	Tuesday	Wednesday	Thursday	Friday	Saturday
		1 ✓ Early Achievements 9am	2 ✓ Early Achievements 9am	3 ✓ ABA 2pm-4pm	4 ✓	5 ✓ ABA 9-11am
6 ✓ ABA 9-11am	7 ✓ Early Achievements 9am	8 ✓ Early Achievements 9am	9 ✓ Early Achievements 9am	10 ✓ Early Achievements 9am	11 ✓ ABA 2pm-4pm	12 ✓ ABA 9-11am
13 ✓ ABA 9-11am	14 ✓ Early Achievements 9am	15 ✓ Early Achievements 9am	16 ✓ Early Achievements 9am	17 ✓ ABA 2pm-4pm	18 ✓ ABA 2pm-4pm	19 ✓ ABA 9-11am
20 ✓ ABA 9-11am	21 ✓ ABA 130pm-330pm Jay's 1st wellness visit	22 ✓ ABA 10am-12pm	23 ✓ ABA 230pm-430pm	24 ✓ ABA 430pm-630pm	25 ✓ ABA 2pm-4pm	26 ✓ ABA 9-11am
27 ✓ ABA 2pm-4pm	28 ✓ ABA 2pm-4pm	29 ✓ ABA 10am-12pm	30 ✓ ABA 10am-12pm	31 ✓ ABA 2pm-4pm Jay's school registration		

September   2017

Title

Subtitle

Sunday	Monday	Tuesday	Wednesday	Thursday	Friday	Saturday
					1 ✓ ABA 2pm-4pm	**2** ✓ ABA 9-11am
3 ✓ ABA 9-11am	**4** ✓ School 9-1135am ✓ Early Achievements 1pm-330pm	**5** ✓ School 9-1135am ✓ Early Achievements 1pm-330pm	**6** ✓ School 9-1135am ✓ Early Achievements 1pm-330pm ✓ ABA 4pm-545pm	**7** ✓ School 9-1135am ✓ Early Achievements 1pm-330pm ✓ ABA 4pm-545pm	**8** ✓ School 9-1135am ✓ ABA 2.30pm-5pm	**9** ✓ ABA 9-11am
10 ✓ ABA 9-11am	**11** ✓ School 9-1135am ✓ Early Achievements 1pm-330pm ✓ Jays back to sch..ng	**12** ✓ School 9-1135am ✓ Early Achievements 1pm-330pm	**13** ✓ School 9-1135am ✓ Early Achievements 1pm-330pm	**14** ✓ School 9-1135am ✓ Early Achievements 1pm-330pm ✓ ABA 4pm-545pm	**15** ✓ School 9-1135am ✓ ABA 2.30pm-5pm	**16** ✓ ABA 9-11am
17 ✓ ABA 9-11am	✓ School 9-1135am ✓ Early Achievements 1pm-330pm	✓ School 9-1135am ✓ Early Achievements 1pm-330pm	✓ School 9-1135am ✓ Early Achievements 1pm-330pm	✓ School 9-1135am ✓ Early Achievements 1pm-330pm ✓ ABA 4pm-545pm	**22** ✓ School 9-1135am ✓ ABA 2.30pm-5pm	**23** ✓ ABA 9-11am
24 ✓ ABA 9-11am	✓ School 9-1135am ✓ Early Achievements 1pm-330pm	✓ School 9-1135am ✓ Early Achievements 1pm-330pm	✓ School 9-1135am ✓ Early Achievements 1pm-330pm	✓ School 9-1135am ✓ Early Achievements 1pm-330pm ✓ ABA 4pm-545pm	**29** ✓ School 9-1135am ✓ ABA 2.30pm-5pm	**30** ✓ ABA 9-11am

Jayson was discharged from Infants and Toddlers in July 2017, and my husband and I made the decision to begin an in-classroom IEP. Jayson started the Early Achievements program at Kennedy Krieger that summer, and the ABA assessment was completed by an organization called Humanim, based in Baltimore. In addition to those services, Jayson also started outpatient speech services at Charm City Therapy, and his schedule was full.

Now the best part of all of this, which was truly a blessing, was the fact that Jayson had the energy to keep going. He had extremely long days for a three-year-old (as shown in the calendars above), but to him he felt like he was playing, though he was learning. Some evenings when ABA came, I felt like crying because he looked so tired from all the other activities he participated in earlier that day, but he stuck with it, and I thank the staff for being patient and doing the activities he loved the most.

In August 2017, my husband and I enrolled Jayson at his Pre-K home-school nearby that offered special education services, and he attended that from 9:00 to 11:30 a.m. Monday through Friday.

First day of school of picture:

AND
Wait for it . . . .
Him getting off the bus in the afternoon!

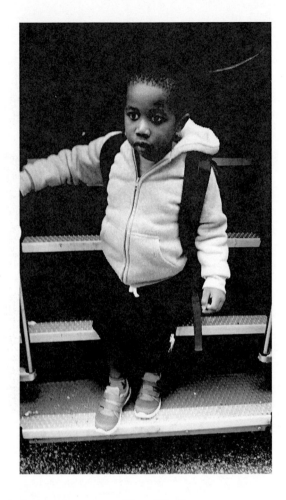

More information regarding the classroom:

If your family decides to go with the IEP option (classroom), and you choose to send your child off to school, you are given the option of either sending them to an exclusion or an inclusion classroom. Exclusion means not being around "typically functioning" peers, and inclusion means that your child will be in a regular classroom with those who might also be autistic *and* those who are "typically functioning" of the same age.

For us, we had to evaluate what was best for Jayson at the time. We considered his weaknesses and strengths, what he could and couldn't do, and since language, expression, talking/speaking/vocalization were NOT going on at all with him, we decided to do an exclusion classroom. This process of evaluating Jayson was another challenge for me. Besides the fact that our marriage was already going through so much already, I felt like my husband wasn't really involved in a lot of the decisions we had to make regarding Jayson. I was in a great state of sadness, confusion, and regret, and then came:

Notes

Phase 4) DEPRESSION. My companions, I know you all will understand this as well. Being able to see the deficits or challenges of your kiddo as compared to the other kids can sometimes bring tears to your eyes. It is so hard to accept that, though there is a challenge right in front of you, you can't take a magic wand like in the movies and make it disappear, make it go away, and make it alright.

I remember so clearly one day working with a client in the library. I started to recall what Jayson was going through, the frustrations he might feel when wanting to say something and not being able to say it or trying to ask another kid to play with him and not knowing how. I sat in the corner of the library and wept like a child. I texted my baby sister, while still crying, that I was crying and sad and depressed and that I had been feeling like this for a while. I told her that though some days I felt strong, I was so weak and didn't know what else to do. My sister quickly got all my other siblings on the phone, and they all encouraged me and "hugged" me from far away. There is nothing like support from your loved ones. I was so saddened about what Jayson was going through that, at times, all I could do was cry.

While in this stage as a side note, my companions, I would like to discuss a few battles Jayson experienced and continues to struggle with at times up to this moment. He experienced these not only in this phase, but from denial up until even now while I am writing this to you. I know that each of our kiddos have some similarities in speech difficulties, but in sensory or behavior areas, I am sure they are quite different. In the past, other families have told me that their kiddo only eats certain types of food, causing eating/nutrition/diet to be extremely hard because of the texture of the food or maybe the temperature at which it's being served. Another difficulty might be that the kiddo doesn't wear certain types of materials or textures. For some families, elopement (wandering off) is a big issue. For others, their kiddos are always having to sleep with a weighted blanket, or some have difficulties falling asleep at all. Recently, a family shared with me that their kiddo has a hard time wearing tight or fitted clothing that touches her skin, so they struggle in the winter when she wears dresses with no tights or leggings and goes outside when it's twenty degrees with no jacket. Seizures are also something that some of our kiddos experience. Difficulties at doctors' appointments (especially at the dentist's office), grooming for our boys (haircuts are an all-day job), and there are other difficulties that I have not even mentioned. All these struggles are real but can be overcome, and we will later go into details about how we can approach them.

My companions, as I share these hardships, only those who are going through this journey like us or have gone through it already can truly understand what other parents with autistic children go through. I know and understand that teachers, speech pathologists, occupational therapists, therapeutic assistants, and ABA technicians have also helped in the process of "tolerating" our children, but we are the ones who live with them, day in and day out. We are the ones who drive everywhere for all sorts of therapies. We endure sleepless nights, night after night. We are the ones who beg for even one day to just go in a cave and turn the knob so that we can have peace and quiet, even for one hour. In Jayson's case, besides the speech difficulties, there were also sensory, elopement, and toilet struggles. Below are the most difficult ones I wanted to share with you all.

The first issue that Jayson had difficulty with happened because he liked (and still likes) to jump and needed pressure on his feet. He would jump from the dining room table to the floor and would also bounce from one couch to the next. By the time he turned two, our couches had had enough and we bought a little indoor trampoline. Though this helped a little, Jayson still wasn't getting high enough from the bounce or getting the sensory input he needed, so he went back to the couch and continues to do so to this day. We've had to repair our couch sets rather than buy new ones.

One day after getting groceries, I wanted to grab a bite to eat. I was craving Chipotle and that's all I wanted. Now, companions, you all know how ridiculous their lines can be at times. After arriving there, the line was long, but I was trying to wait a little for the line to go down a bit. I waited and waited, but more people kept coming. I eventually went in with Jayson, but let me keep it real for a moment, I contemplated leaving him in the car, and I know you parents have thought the exact same thing once in a while. I also thought to myself, 'I don't want anyone calling the cops on me and dragging me to jail, only for Chipotle.'

When we entered, he did pretty well in the beginning. I gave him my phone and he waited patiently. Unfortunately, there was one lady in front of us who wanted to place a big order, and in my mind I was like, 'OMG, seriously!' So we ended up being in there for a while, and during that time I debated whether or not we should leave, but I hung in there. They eventually started my order, and that's when all hell broke loose. Jayson showed off! He wanted to run and touch everything. You parents know that there are some days that you feel like explaining to others what your child is going through and other days, you are just not in the mood. You sometimes feel that you shouldn't have to explain what's happening, but at that moment, you are trying to justify to those around you that your child is not a "bad" child, but rather that they have behavioral difficulties, in hopes that other people will not think you are a bad parent or that you don't discipline your children at home.

One lady was looking at me like I was the worst mother on the face of this earth, wondering why I was not disciplining him or correcting his behavior (we will discuss the topic of discipline later). I got my order and we left, and I quickly called my younger sister to explain everything. The one thing I love most about my baby sister is her compassion and the understanding heart she has towards others. The minute I finished telling her my story, she quickly apologized as if she did something wrong. She felt so bad. I told her, "I wish there were things that could make it easier for us parents that allow us to not have to wait in line for anything." So she mentioned to me about Uber Eats and a few other apps that allow you to order food for pick-up or delivery.

Besides this, there is so much convenience now with grocery stores and restaurants that will allow you to place your order and pick it up by the curb without getting out of the car. I used to think that those people were so lazy and, now, with what I've experienced, I don't judge or take anything at face value anymore. I also used to be one of those people who wondered why parents would not discipline their children whether at home or in public, not knowing that I didn't have wisdom to understand that I was the one who was ignorant. Like the Bible says, "Do not judge others and you will not be judged," (Matthew 7:1) and furthermore, "Don't speak evil against each other, dear brothers and sisters. If you criticize and judge each other, then you are criticizing and judging God's law. But your job is to obey the law, not to judge whether it applies to you" (James 4:11). Through this experience with Jayson, I have had to go to the Father and ask for help and understanding several times, and His word states: "If you need wisdom, ask our generous God, and he will give it to you. He will not rebuke you for asking" (James 1:5).

From this incident moving forward, I understood more

when I saw a child acting out in public or having a tantrum, it wasn't just for nothing because my child taught me a lesson that faithful day. Hosea 4:6 tells us that "My {God's} people are destroyed for lack of knowledge," and I was no longer uninformed from that day forth.

The last and most difficult battle Jayson experienced was one that I would like to address later during my discussion on understanding hardships, trials, and the importance of prayers. As I wrapped up this phase of depression, I told myself that these needed to be my last tears! I told myself that I was getting Jayson the help he needed to get through this part of his life. I had to get a hold of myself and my emotions. From that day forward, I didn't want to turn back to crying. I didn't want to turn back to regrets. I didn't want to turn back to feeling bad for Jayson. I didn't want to think that I wasn't doing my part for him. That day, I cried my last tears for Jayson and finally moved on to Phase 5: Acceptance!

To move forward:

- Cry, cry, and take deep breaths.
- Seek additional support, whether in your circle or out.
- See a therapist if necessary.
- Continue with intervention for your kiddo.
- Finally accept that these are (hopefully!) your last tears.
- **MOVE FORWARD!**

Let me finish my thoughts regarding the classroom discussion. For your kiddo, it might be different. Your kiddo might speak or have a few words so they could benefit from being around others who are speaking in order to get them to keep vocalizing. But in Jayson's case, we just felt that he would be so lost in that classroom of maybe eighteen or more kids. However, in the exclusion classroom that we visited, there was a special education teacher and three assistants who were in the classroom daily. In addition, the exclusion class included a weekly session with a speech pathologist and an occupational therapist. Though the classroom increases in size throughout the year (because once a child turns three, they are allowed to start school), the teacher is allowed to ask for more assistants if they see fit. In Jayson's classroom in August 2017, there were six kids who started and by June 2018, there were eleven kids. To us, that was better than eighteen to twenty-three children.

For more information and to explore your options, I encourage you to visit lovin' adoptin' supporting adoptive parents and families living with Autism at https://lovinadoptin. com/ as you start to make your decisions on which path to take for your kiddo. That's enough about Jayson for now, but we will talk about him more later.

"Go in peace," the priest replied. "For the Lord is watching over your journey."

—*Judges 18:6*

Notes

Diagnosis of ASD and My Relationship with GOD

"Search me, O God, and know my heart, test me and know my anxious thoughts."

—*Psalms 139:23*

B EFORE I DISCUSS the final phase of acceptance, my dear companions, I want you all to understand that, just like each of our journeys with our kiddos is different, our progression through each phase will also be different. You might go right through from denial straight to acceptance, and some of you might start from depression and go right into acceptance, and others might go from denial to anger to bargaining back again to denial, then bargaining again before moving to depression. This will be different for each of us, and that's okay. The most important thing, my companions, is that I would love to see ALL of us reach acceptance!

Phase 5) ACCEPTANCE. This part will be my favorite part of the book because it is coming from my heart. Not to say that the other parts don't mean anything or are not coming from the heart, but it shows you my nakedness. It shows you at my most vulnerable. It shows you at the lowest point in my life, and most of all, it shows you at my weakest, because at my weakest point, GOD is the most POWERFUL! 2 Corinthians 12:9-10 says, "*My grace is all you need. My power works best in weakness. So now I am glad to boast about my weaknesses, so that the power of Christ can work through me. That's why I take pleasure in my weaknesses, and in the insults, hardships, persecutions, and troubles that I suffer for Christ. For when I am weak, then I am strong.*" Most of us have heard that you cannot have a testimony without a test, and this is so true. In my life, up to this point, I was never tested, until we received Jayson's diagnosis of autism. I had just been "going with the flow." I heard of GOD, I believed He existed, I knew there was a higher power, but I didn't really KNOW KNOW HIM and didn't have a RELATIONSHIP with HIM. I didn't know HIM intimately like HE knew me. And at times, GOD has to knock us down a couple of inches, meters, or even feet to get your attention. This time around, HE certainly got my attention.

After the diagnosis, I had some good days, some rough days, and some really, really bad days. I had some up-and-down days, some sleepless nights, and some nights where I fell asleep crying by myself. I mean, I went through *a lot*. And I think at times that is how GOD wants us to feel so that we totally depend on HIM and HIM alone. I was completely helpless. I couldn't fix this. I couldn't take this, or ask this person, or make this phone call for this problem to go away. It wasn't an overnight fix, and that killed me because people who know me best would tell anyone that I am a fixer. It is my personality to fix things. I don't like having too many projects without an end goal or a solution; therefore, this one took a lot out of me. I needed to really depend on GOD.

Through my years of reading books or novels, I remember a remark that President John F. Kennedy once made: "When

written in Chinese, the word 'crisis' is composed of two
characters. One represents danger, and the other represents
opportunity." Every crisis is, at the same time, an opportunity.
Crises are often caused by unexpected difficulties. In this
situation, I could look at it with anger and quit or I could look
at it as an opportunity and challenge myself for growth in the
Lord. In my head, I had to relinquish my power and allow
GOD's power to really fix this situation, which was really hard
for me.

So, I had to start somewhere. I had to first accept who Christ
was over again and who GOD the FATHER is, and I started
reading His Word daily. I even went as far as challenging myself
to read the Bible in one year, something I had never done in my
life. I started the Bible in One Year plan by Nicky and Pippa
Gumbel. The outline of the plan was a daily commentary/
devotional, a New Testament text, an Old Testament text, a
Psalm, and a Proverb. One thing I quickly understood from
Nicky was this: "Regret looks back. Fear looks around. Worry
looks in. Faith looks up." I had to look UP! I had enough with
regret, fear, and worry. It was time for FAITH!

I had to change my mindset in order to "accept" this new
normal, and that didn't mean accepting that my child's life
would be like this forever, but rather that I needed to depend
on GOD for healing and restoration *for* my child! More
importantly, His Word tells us in Isaiah 55:8-9 that "My
thoughts are nothing like your thoughts," says the Lord. "And
my ways are far beyond anything you could imagine. For just
as the heavens are higher than the earth, so my ways are higher
than your ways and my thoughts higher than your thoughts."
So I knew that ultimately GOD knew I needed HIS guidance,
grace, mercy, strength, and power to move forward with what
I was about to face. More importantly, HE reminds us further
down in Isaiah 55:11 that "It is the same with my word. I send

it out, and it always produces fruit. It will accomplish all I want it to, and it will prosper everywhere I send it." What a great feeling and privilege it is to serve someone who loves us and reassures us that HIS Word never fails and that no matter what comes out of HIS mouth, it will do what HE means for it to do, no matter what. Now, my companions, that's our Creator, Problem Solver, Savior, King of Kings, Lord of Lords, and our GREAT, I AM!

My mountain of a challenge of reading the Bible in one year was finding a way to begin that transition. For there to be real change in your life, your mindset has to change. There was a reading one day in which Nicky focused on the need for new clothes and the need for changing old clothes. He stated:

> As well as the outer clothing, our hearts and minds have an inner clothing. When you come into a relationship with God through Jesus, the old clothes have to go and you need a new set of clothes for your heart and mind.

This statement really touched me. I knew I had gone through a transformation, I knew my mind and heart had changed, but I needed to wake up every day knowing that I had thrown away and burned those old clothes and that they were nowhere to be found. I needed to keep reminding myself that the devil would not take me back to that place of feeling alone and blaming GOD for what was happening with my child or feeling worthless for not being able to "fix" the situation.

In all, I had to remind myself of two things: Psalms 55:22, which instructs us to *"give your burdens to the Lord, and He will take care of you. He will not permit the godly to slip and fall,"* and, as Pippa perfectly puts it:

Trust is being able to let go and give oneself, or a situation, over to God, without holding back. It is a child in a parent's arms, never doubting for a moment that they are safe.

I was in my FATHER's arms, and what a great place to be!

I remember at the beginning of my faith journey, I think I still had some doubt that GOD would really heal our child. As you parents are already aware of and understand, I was doing so much running and taking Jayson here and there with so many appointments that I was not doing anything for myself. I think back on what Nicky Gumbel said, "So often, it is our struggles rather than our 'successes' that makes us stronger," and I definitely believe that this "minor setback" really made me stronger. The funny thing is that it didn't matter that everything was about Jayson because I wasn't someone who was about going out with friends or taking trips, so my life didn't really change. Everything had become about Jayson at all costs because he needed the most help, and I needed to be his voice since he didn't have one. When you focus so much of your energy on one child, the other child (ren) can become unfortunate casualties. We will dive in deeper into the impact on siblings later. I fought so hard for our child and I still do that today. But there is a difference now. Another touching statement that Nicky made during one of our daily Bible readings was:

Don't be afraid of pressure. Pressure is what transforms a lump of coal into a diamond. Life can be seen as a series of tests. We test things by putting them under pressure. Physical muscles grow through being put under pressure. God is more interested in how your heart and mind grow when they are tested.

This was one of those tests that I didn't want to fail, and I wanted my heart and mind to grow in and with HIM.

As one grows in dependence on GOD, we need to let HIM have it all. You have to let Him have it and you can't decide to keep any part of it, but most importantly, like Nicky states, you have to "realize how big God is and how small our problems are in comparison with His power." I remember when I was working on getting to know GOD more, my older sister called me just to check on the kids. She asked how Jayson was doing, and I said he was doing well and we were seeing signs of improvement. I told her that I was feeling really tired from always driving him somewhere. My sister told me to please be careful and not turn Jayson into an idol. I stayed quiet and remembered back in the Old Testament when people were worshiping other gods and I thought to myself, 'Oh my goodness, I hope I am not doing that.' After we got off the phone, I pondered on that statement and knew I had to make some changes. I would never want my Father to think I would put our son before HIM. Inasmuch as I knew Jayson needed my help, I also knew that Philippians 4:6 says, *"Don't worry about anything; instead, pray about everything. Tell God what you need, and thank him for all he has done."* I knew I had to start thanking Him more and letting more go and letting GOD do more!

In February 2017, my mother introduced me to a cousin of mine who at the time was residing in Cameroon and was on fire for GOD. As an individual who really struggles with meeting new people and exposing herself to others, this was really hard for me. I am not one to seek out relationships; I guess I am unique in that way. But I am someone who loves being alone in a quiet place. I also struggled with the idea of having to explain to others what is "wrong" with my child. Now, you parents also understand what I am talking about. But it is such a struggle having to explain to others why your child does things repeatedly or why he goes in circles or why he is frequently jumping. Some days, we feel like explaining, and other days we don't, and that's just a fact. Nonetheless, I gave this relationship a chance and by the grace of GOD, my relationship with GOD drastically changed. As we started talking, this cousin of mine made me aware of his many gifts and how he drew nigh to GOD. Throughout the conversation, he never openly told me he was a prophet, but I could sense it because he interpreted and explained a lot of things to me that the Holy Spirit was telling him. The beauty of meeting a prophet is that you don't have to reveal too much. They are the ones who reveal things to you instead, in order to prove to us that GOD does truly still have prophets here on earth. When we started talking, this person exposed so much to me about myself, my marriage, Jayson, etc. Imagine that this person calls me to pray for Jayson and instead ends up praying for me because at that time I was having severe hemorrhoid pain.

Okay, ladies (sorry gentlemen), let me drop a little TMI. We all know pregnancy changes your body from the inside out, literally! When I tell you the thing I hated most with pregnancy was hemorrhoids, I am NOT lying! I suffered hemorrhoids in both of my pregnancies, but it seemed even worse during and after my pregnancy with Jayson. I had tried everything over the counter and nothing was working. No cream, ointment, hot/cold compress, suppository, Tucks pads, soaking in the tub in warm or hot water was helping the situation in any way. The only thing that gave me a little relief was aloe vera (the actual plant). I would drink it (extremely bitter) and apply some to the area daily, but I was still in pain and wondered how long I had to do this and if I had to live this way for the rest of my life. Since I was still doing a lot of running around with Jayson and I couldn't frequently use public restrooms, the situation quickly became unbearable! In short, I was running short on time and was going through some really bad days and was just about to schedule surgery in a few days. When I spoke to that cousin of mine, he told me to put my hands on that particular area where I was having the pain, and he prayed and prayed. Within three days, I tell you all as my close companions, it's as though I had forgotten I was in pain or that I was even going through what I just mentioned above. The pain literally disappeared without me knowing. The intercession that my cousin did for my chronic pain amazed me so much, I wanted to have faith in God like that . . . for Jayson.

From that week on, he and I started doing Bible studies twice a week. We addressed different topics, and I was puzzled by who GOD really was and is! The perspective he gave me about who GOD is opened my eyes and I couldn't stop seeking HIS face daily. At times, we must realize that there are some people who only draw themselves closer to GOD by physically experiencing HIS healing power or HIS restoration or HIS redemption, and once they come out on the other side, they are able to now proclaim victory about what GOD did for them. This is all fine, but at times GOD wants us to have that faith knowing HE will do it because HE loves His children and always will; however, Romans 8:17 states *"and since we are his children, we are his heirs. In fact, together with Christ we are heirs of God's glory. But if we are to share his glory, we must also share his suffering."* We must all remember what Christ did for us on that cross! Therefore, because of my healing, I knew GOD can, could, and will heal and restore Jayson to perfect health as well!

During those appointment times with Jayson, other parents would tell me that they saw signs, but I didn't "see" any signs, and I have worked with that population for a few years. It was therefore amazing to my surprise that GOD would bring that right to my own doorstep, and even more, HE brought it into my household. But you know what, I have learned through reading the Word that HE states, *"And I will give you treasures hidden in the darkness—secret riches. I will do this so you may know that I am Lord, the God of Israel, the one who calls you by name."* Therefore, if HE knows me by name, HE has better plans for me and knows why He is doing what HE is doing, and though we will all go through trials and tribulations in life, HE will always give us solutions to every problem. By reading His Word, you will come to realize that it has solutions for anger, anxiety, hopelessness, weight, pride, fear, diseases, sexuality, parental guidance, marriage, dating, everyday living, etc. However, today I want to reassure you that you can win those battles, and furthermore, 1 Corinthians 2:9 states, *"No eye has seen, no ear has heard, and no mind has imagined what God has prepared for those who love Him."* So I will keep loving and trusting Him, for only HE knows the plans HE has for Jayson's life.

Notes

The Holy Spirit

As I continued to work on my relationship with GOD, my cousin and I then moved to doing Bible study to once a week where we would target certain topics like angels, anger, taking up your cross, keys to gates, the importance of prayer, who Jesus is, the Holy Spirit, etc. Before going into the topic of the Holy Spirit, my companions, I want you all to know that GOD is three things: HE is Omnipotent (all powerful), Omniscient (all-knowing), and Omnipresent (all-present). So we can ask, how can HE be present everywhere all the time and be anywhere all the time? My dear companions, that's where the beautiful gift of the HOLY SPIRIT comes in! We thank HIM for HIS angels who are always watching us, but the Holy Spirit enables and empowers us even more throughout every situation in life to know He will never leave us. I like even more what Nicky Gumbel states:

> We have the extraordinary privilege of living in the age of the Spirit. God's law is not simply written on tablets of stone. Rather, God works in you, by his Spirit, to give you a passion to please him. . . . As you pray, the Holy Spirit, who lives in you, helps you to pray. It is an extraordinary privilege to be living in this time when every Christian has the Holy Spirit living within them. Before the day of Pentecost, the Holy Spirit only came on particular people at particular times for particular tasks.

Like GOD's word states in Hebrews 10:16: "This is the new covenant I will make with my people on that day, says the LORD: I will put my laws in their hearts, and I will write them on their minds." Thank you, Lord!

One thing we must understand as we start building our faith

is that we are not alone. Though we can't see GOD or physically touch Him, He is right there. He wants us to come to Him and be in His midst. He wants to hear our laughter, our sadness, and our tears. When we laugh, He laughs; when we cry, He cries. Therefore, He wants us to know that He is always right there with us when we might feel any of those emotions previously mentioned. But He also wants us to humble ourselves and know that, though He told us there will be problems in life, He will be right there with us every step of the way. Out of every test in our lives, we must come on the other side with a testimony to glorify our God! To show others that He is who He says He really is, you must believe. You must let go. You must trust. You must surrender. You must have faith. You must want to follow His will for your life.

Jeremiah 29:11 states: "'For I know the plans I have for you,' says the Lord, 'they are plans for good and not for disaster, to give you a future and a hope.'" Therefore, we must know, my dear companions that our Father will never give us things that frustrate us or make us mad or make us cry. So, let's let all that go and know that GOD has a great plan for our lives and our children's lives, not only for the now, but also for the future.

Remember, though we can't see GOD, He is still right here. I will say it again that the Holy Spirit is GOD's presence within us, which is why He will never leave us. And this is what the Holy Spirit is: "... this kind of fruit in our lives; love, joy, peace, patience, kindness, goodness, faithfulness," according to Galatians 5:22, so we have nothing to worry about and nothing to fear.

Though I have grown in my faith in GOD, there are still moments when the devil tries to get in my mind to control my thoughts, which is why most of the battles we face are in our minds! Once we correct our minds as previously mentioned and gain control of our thoughts, things tend to take a shift.

I always recommend to new Christians or even those who have been Christians for a while to read Joyce Meyer's book *Battlefield of the Mind*. This book's goal is to help readers change their lives by improving their daily thoughts. Meyer focuses on worry, doubt, confusion, depression, anger, and feelings of condemnation and states that these are all attacks on the mind and encourages readers who suffer from negative thoughts to take heart and to get in control of their minds.

Right now, we are all in a war that some might be aware of and others might not be aware of. As long as we are alive, we will always be in a middle of a war, and the goal is not to become of this world. As Billy Graham states: "Whatever you love most, be it sports, pleasure, business, or God, that is your god!" (Neill, 1984, as cited in Gumbel, 2018). The constant temptation of the world is to divide our hearts, and we must do our best to resist and stop chasing the things of this world by living not in the flesh, but in the spirit. As Joyce Meyer states:

> Every one of us needs to continuously make adjustments to put our fleshly desires under the Holy Spirit's control and not let our emotions or mind rule us. Scripture explains that the spirit wars against the flesh and the flesh wars against the spirit, so they are continually antagonistic toward each other.

Once we can be in control of our thoughts, the Bible has solutions to many storms we might face, and it is our goal now to go into prayer to fight these battles we are facing. 1 Corinthians 2:13-14 states ". . . we do not use words that come from human wisdom. Instead, we speak words given to us by the Spirit, using the Spirit's words given to us to explain spiritual truths. But people who aren't spiritual can't receive these truths from God's Spirit. It all sounds foolish to them and they can't understand it, for only those who are spiritual can understand what the spirit means."

As we start to understand the things of the Spirit and this gift GOD gave us, we will begin to understand how we can better pray for our children who are battling this crisis. Joyce Meyer later concludes:

It's a war! The devil hates us, and he is constantly working overtime trying to make sure that we give in to the flesh. Ultimately, you decide who wins in your life. You don't have to be subject to your flesh. You can live in the Spirit, bringing your flesh in line with His (GOD's) Will.

You, too, can win the battle today. We definitely can win the battle today over autism, "for the word of God will never fail" (Luke 1:37).

Notes

The importance and power of prayers (in line with God's will)

My companions, prayer is something that up until this moment in my life, I am still working on. It is something that is so important, simple, but requires such dedication, desire, and discipline. It is our time with GOD, not only to list to HIM the desires of our hearts (which He already knows), but for HIM to speak back to us (the most important part). When we go to our Father, our Creator, our Maker, our Daddy, our Provider, our King of Kings, our Lord of Lords—we must go to Him with expectancy that HE will respond back to us, but we also have to be willing to take the time to *listen* and *pay attention* to HIS soft sound.

As I continued to work on my faith building through the months and years, it really took me a while to grasp the understanding that I must make time for GOD. I must be in HIS presence and give HIM time to speak back to me after I have gone through my list of struggles and things I need guidance from HIM for and what I need HIM to intervene on. I was able to do some devotions on how to hear from GOD and when to know it's HIM who is speaking to you. The Holy Spirit guided me on how to know when our HEAVENLY FATHER was speaking to me and how to go about things regarding myself and Jayson.

So, as I started to pray, most of the devotions I read to build my faith focused on acronyms that helped me while praying in order for me not to forget something. These have stayed with me during moments when I feel like slacking off; after all, I am human! There are days that you just don't feel like spending time with GOD in "prayer." Therefore, we can go to our LORD and offer a moment of thanksgiving, worship, and praise through songs.

Before addressing how we can pray, we need to address what we are up against. Throughout the New Testament, primarily in the Gospels, we hear a lot about how Jesus was going around with His disciples healing women, men, and children from all types of sicknesses and diseases. That same healing Jesus possessed back then is still possible today through the power HE has given us. However, before we can call upon CHRIST for healing, there are a few things we need to understand about the world we live in. There was one devotion that I did during my earlier months when I started studying the Word with my cousin. It was a five-day devotion titled *The Armor of God*. In this devotion, Priscilla Shirer goes into detail about all-day, every-day, invisible wars around us—unseen, unheard, yet felt throughout every aspect of our lives. She goes into depth about the goals of the devil/enemy wreaking havoc on everything that matters to you (i.e., your heart, your mind, your marriage, your children, your relationships, your dreams, your destiny, etc.) and making sure he (the devil) catches you unaware and unarmed. Shirer goes on to describe how to put on the full armor of GOD and put into action plans and strategies that can secure us the VICTORY through GOD's WORD!

My companions, let me first discuss what the armor of GOD is. The armor of GOD is the way GOD wants us to enter into battle each day because HE knows what we are up against. HE tells us there is a certain wardrobe to put on in order to defeat those attacks that come our way unexpectedly from the devil and the "world." As we wake up in the morning, we must be mindful to suit up and put that armor on. The Bible lists these components in Ephesians 6:10-18:

> Finally, be strong in the Lord and in his mighty power.
> Put on the full armor of God so that you can take your
> stand against the devil's schemes. For our struggle is not

against flesh and blood, but against the rulers, against the authorities, against the powers of this dark world and against the spiritual forces of evil in the heavenly realms. Therefore, put on the full armor of God, so that when the day of evil comes, you may be able to stand your ground, and after you have done everything, to stand. Stand firm then, with the belt of truth (HE alone is the truth of life—spend time in His Word and learn His truth) buckled around your waist, with the breastplate of righteousness (thank GOD for His mercy upon us and the life of His Son Jesus so that we could spend eternity with Him) in place, and with your feet fitted with the readiness that comes from the gospel of peace. In addition to all this, take up the shield of faith (this guard against the constant assaults by the enemy), with which you can extinguish all the flaming arrows of the evil one. Take the helmet of salvation (this protects us once we accept Jesus Christ as our Lord and Savior) and the sword of the Spirit (reading your Bible, learning His Word and memorizing verses. Keep it on the tip of your tongue), which is the word of God. And pray in the Spirit on all occasions with all kinds of prayers and requests. With this in mind, be alert and always keep on praying for all the saints. {block indentation}

The first day of the devotion focuses primarily on the book of Ephesians. Shirer begins by telling us that:

the most troubling things in your life—things you perceive with your five physical senses—are not real issues. Everything that occurs in the visible, *physical world* is directly connected to the wrestling match being waged in the *invisible spiritual world*. Your real enemy- the devil -wants you to ignore the spiritual reality behind the physical one. Because as long as you're focused on what you can *see* with your physical eyes, he can continue to run rampant underneath the surface. {block indentation}

My companions, I really want you all to understand this long statement. I want you all to absorb and take this all in in order for us to move forward. To sum it up, the real battles that we have in life are not the things we see with our physical eyes. Rather what the devil does under the surface is what is causing havoc in our lives, and the more he keeps us busy thinking that the only real thing is what we see, he will always try to win. Shirer continues to state that "the more you disregard him, the more damage he is free to do . . . he is very real and very persistent waging war against us constantly."

While on this topic, in the next few paragraphs, I would like to finally discuss the hardest battle that came with this diagnosis that I briefly mentioned at the last part of the depression phase. I needed to bring this battle into this section only because this battle needed real intercession from others. Intercessory prayers are the ones you pray on behalf of someone else or someone else prays on your behalf; however, to receive them means that you will have to expose the most intimate things in your household that are supposed to be covered by the roof of your house. This was hard on Jayson but also very difficult for my husband and me because we are from a different culture. It was hard to embrace the idea of letting others into our private lives, especially my husband, who finds privacy extremely important for keeping life and marriage sacred or exclusive. I know most of you will understand where I am coming from and would like to shed tears as I talk about this battle, but I am not telling you this to make you cry, but to inform you about what a MIGHTY GOD we serve. HE truly deserves ALL the glory and praise and as I write this today, I decree and declare "that at the name of Jesus every knee should bow, in heaven and on earth and under earth, and every tongue declare that Jesus Christ is Lord, to the Glory of God the Father." (Philippians 2:10-11) "Are any of you suffering hardships? You should pray. Are any of you happy? You should sing praises." (James 5:13)

The last and the most difficult battle Jayson had at home was between the ages of two and three. When he would have a bowel movement, he first started to play with it and then it progressed into eating it. Yes, my companions, you read that correctly—he was eating his own feces. This was the hardest and saddest part of my life because this was one of those things about which I know I definitely needed PRAYERS! I couldn't understand how someone could have a bowel movement and then take that and put it into their mouth to eat. If I tell you I was devastated, I was truly devastated. My companions, this particular battle kept me going back from anger to depression during my coping phases for a long time. I was helping and encouraging other parents, but inside of my household, I was going through this demonic hold on my child that I couldn't comprehend.

Besides that cousin of mine who was praying for and with me, I also met a few other ladies who interceded in prayers for Jayson in such a huge way that I will never forget. These individuals interceded for us, and by the time I looked up or around, Jayson had stopped eating his feces. I had to go back again and thank GOD truly for who HE was and what HE was doing in the life of Jayson. Scriptures reminds us ". . . the Holy Spirit helps us in our weakness. For example, we don't know what God wants us to pray for. But the Holy Spirit prays for us with groanings that cannot be expressed in words" (Romans 8:26). The Scriptures also instruct us to "Give all your worries and cares to God, for He cares about you" (1 Peter 5:7).

With this battle that we as Christians or non-Christians are up against, Paul, the writer of Ephesians, tells us the only way we can defeat the enemy is through the power of prayer and that's the armor to put on! Paul draws us to pay attention to the spiritual battles that exist in the invisible, unseen realm, primarily to show us the power that each of us possesses because of our relationship with GOD through Christ Jesus! As we build our relationship with GOD, He will equip us with gifts that will enable us to know when the devil is trying to sneak an attack our way.

Shirer continues to day two and educates us that Paul taught us in Ephesians 6 that as we start to build this relationship with GOD "the first step for us in utilizing the spiritual resources we've been given is to have our spiritual eyes opened so that we can see them." Furthermore, she states that "you cannot use them if you're not aware of their availability and their importance in successfully waging war against the enemy. Victory starts here. It starts today. It starts with a prayer for vision."

As we move to day 3, Shirer focuses on staying on what is true in order to not be thrown off course as she reminds us that "the devil's packaging is so clever that unless we know what's true—I mean really know it, know it at our core—we easily fall prey to his ploys." We need to remind ourselves, and Shirer teaches us that:

The truth is who God is and what He says it is, which is best summed up for us with the Person of Jesus Christ. God's truth. Biblical truth. Without concrete allegiance to and affirmation with this truth—with real truth—you're left weak and susceptible to things that may look right and sound right yet actually aren't right.

Additionally, Psalms 119:160 tells us "the very essence of your words is truth; all your just regulations will stand forever." On day four of the devotional, Shirer reminds us again that:

The enemy wants to distract you . . . so he can blindside you. And listen to me—he is not indiscriminately shooting these arrows of his . . . he's studied your tendencies and habits, your deepest fears and weaknesses, and has aimed at those areas in particular. He knows he can't destroy you. You're eternally secure in Jesus. But he fully intends to sidetrack your attention by setting any number of internal fires ablaze in your life, like insecurity, intimidation, anxiety, worry or busyness. He wants you to be unfocused while he sneaks up from behind.

The next armor that Paul instructs us to take up is the shield of faith. Paul starts off in Ephesians 6:10-17 stating "A final word: Be strong in the Lord and in his mighty power. Put on all of God's armor so that you will be able to stand firm against all strategies of the devil. For we are not fighting against flesh-and-blood enemies, but against evil rulers and authorities of the unseen world, against mighty powers in this dark world, and against evil spirits in the heavenly places . . . hold up the shield of faith to stop the fiery arrows of the devil. Put on salvation as your helmet, and take the sword of the Spirit, which is the word of God." Therefore, my companions, we are prepared and ready to enter the world. Once we suit up and put this on, we know our LORD has given us the gift to not fall prey to the evil plans of the wicked one. We thank GOD for always thinking of us and providing to us His armor to protect us!

On day five, Shirer ends with defining the final principle of having and keeping faith. Shirer states that "we define faith with this simple meaning: acting like God is telling truth." She continues to state that "the truth of God is what makes having faith in God worth it. Without truth, we have nothing solid to hang our shield of faith on. So knowing the truth of God and the truth about God as revealed in His Word is critical if we want to live out our faith responsibly and experience the benefits of being protected by our shields."

So, we are aware of what the devil does, what he wants us to think and believe, what is not real, but we have also been given the power to overcome his lies and deceits. For us to achieve our purpose, the purpose of our children, and the purpose of our other relationships, we must continually pray and always put on the full armor of GOD! More importantly, we must ". . . .stay alert and be persistent in your prayers for all believers everywhere." (Ephesians 6:18).

Now that I knew what I was up against and how the devil was trying to hold Jayson back from achieving his purpose and destiny in life . . . .

Notes

I had to start praying!

But

I knew I needed to go into it like Nicky states: "Keep your eyes fixed on Jesus. Trust in him. Abide in him. Serve him with all your heart. Live a life of faith. Stay faithful to him and pray faithfully for others. This is the way of true satisfaction. Faith pleases God."

Therefore, I prayed for Jayson, started my prayer list for others around me, especially those kiddos I saw frequently, whether in Jayson's class in school or Kennedy Krieger, and trusted and believed that GOD would touch and heal ALL of our kiddos!

The first acronym I learned for prayer was ACTS:

Adoration—During this moment, you spend time adoring the Lord for who He is, giving thanks to Him for another day, and thanking Him in advance for what He will do.

Confession—Go before the Lord asking for forgiveness for all your sins (those you are aware of and those you are not aware of). Repenting allows you to start afresh, wipes the slate clean, and the Lord wants you to know and reassures you that once you repent He forgets, and you should forget as well because of what His Son Jesus Christ did on the Cross for us!

Thanksgiving—We thank GOD for all He is doing in our lives and in the lives of our family and friends. We thank Him for our health, jobs, marriages, homes, food, children, etc., as well as the new opportunities to come. We thank HIM for loving us despite our many faults and for His lovingkindness that gives us the opportunity to call ourselves His children.

Supplication—This is where you make all your requests known to GOD and just surrender everything. Being open, humble, and committed to come into His presence is what GOD wants from us. James 4:2 says, "You don't have what you want because you don't ask God for it."

Another acronym that helped me become more effective and efficient was P.R.A.Y. As I mentioned before, my prayer life went up and down; however, I worked through it, with dedication, desire, and discipline.

Praise—allows you to come into His presence with praise, singing, and thanksgiving! That's the best way to enter prayer! Psalm 100:1-4 tells us to ". . . .enter into His gates with thanksgiving, and into His courts with praise. Be thankful to Him, and bless His name."

Repent—asking for forgiveness of your sins. Coming before GOD and saying, "LORD, put the spotlight on anything in my life that puts a barrier in my relationship with you and I repent of it." Psalm 19: 12-13 tells us "Who can understand his errors? Cleanse me from secret faults. Keep back your servant also from presumptuous sins; let them not have dominion over me. Then I shall be blameless and I shall be innocent of great transgression." So when you pray, ask GOD to reveal any sin that you might be overlooking, and He will honor your heart of repentance.

Ask—going before our heavenly Father and asking for what we want. GOD loves us and wants the very best for us. Matthew 7:7-8 says "Ask and it will be given to you; seek and you will find; knock, and it will be opened to you. For everyone who asks receives, and he who seeks finds, and to him who knocks it will be opened."

Before we address the letter Y for Yield, Jesus talks to us more about how prayer really works during His last hours with His disciples. Jesus emphasized to them over and over the importance of asking and that God's answers are based on three conditions:

1. John 14:13—Jesus says your requests must glorify GOD. HE states "and whatever you ask in my name, that I will do, that the Father may be glorified in the Son. If you ask anything in my name I will do it."

2. John 15:7—Jesus says that your requests must be in harmony with His Word. "If you abide in me, and my words abide in you, you will ask what you desire and it shall be done for you."

3. John 16:23-24—Jesus tells us that the request must bring you joy. "And in that day you will ask me nothing. Most assuredly, I say to you, whatever you ask the Father in My name He will give you. Until now you have asked nothing in my name. Ask, and you will receive, that your joy may be full."

Ultimately, we see that GOD doesn't want to see us weep over our children. He doesn't want to see us tired and exhausted or not enjoy our children/the fruits of our labor. He doesn't want us to grieve, be mad, depressed, sad, and angry over anything HE meant to be a blessing to us. Therefore, I know autism is not from GOD and that healing can occur if we pray fervently and without ceasing to our mighty GOD! More importantly, I know that 1 Peter 2:24 teaches us that ". . . .by HIS wounds we are healed." Nicky reminds us that "All the hurts we pick up in our lives can be brought to the cross and given to Jesus. We don't need to hold on to the past (or the present). Jesus suffered and died that we might be healed physically, emotionally, spiritually."

Yield—(the hardest part) is when you wait, listen, and seek to hear from GOD. Ask GOD to speak to your heart and HE definitely will; however, you have to be silent before Him. His Word in Psalm 27:14 states: "Wait patiently for the Lord. Be brave and courageous. Yes, wait patiently for the Lord."

So for Jayson, I spent a lot of time with GOD seeking His face by reading His Word! I wanted to feel Him in my presence and hear from Him every moment in my life in order to know right from wrong decisions. I needed to be guided by the Holy Spirit for me to know that I was putting the right people around Jayson who were not hindering his progress but instead helping and encouraging him, but most importantly seeing past his diagnosis. While praying for Jayson, remember, I also tried to intercede for his classmates at school and at Kennedy Krieger because it pleased GOD and I was blessed in the process. I remember there were times during observation days at the achievements program at Kennedy that I would look up in Heaven wishing that GOD Himself would visit us. I would pray that He could appear and heal all our children from their diseases and make all our children speak, for them to no longer have such behavioral difficulties and just be free to worship Him! Oh, how I can't wait for that day!

My cousin also helped me with several prayer points monthly to help me in breaking the chains that were binding Jayson from speaking, and we continue to do this today. An example would be as follows:

PRAYER POINTS FOR JAYSON

- EXODUS 23:25 "Worship the LORD your God, and his blessing will be on your food and water. I will take away sickness from among you."
- ISAIAH 53:5 "But he was pierced for our transgressions, he was crushed for our iniquities; the punishment that brought us peace was on him, and by his wounds we are healed."

PRAYER POINTS

1. Psalm 103:3 "who forgives all your sins and heals all your diseases"; LORD, I BLESS YOUR HOLY NAME FOR YOUR HEALING POWER OVER MY LIFE AND FAMILY, IN JESUS' MIGHTY NAME.

2. Matthew 21:19 "Seeing a fig tree by the road, he went up to it but found nothing on it except leaves. Then he said to it, "May you never bear fruit again!" Immediately the tree withered." LIKE THE FIG TREE, YOU STRANGE AFFLICTION IN THE MOUTH OF JAYSON, BEAR FRUITS NO MORE AND WITHER OUT OF HIS LIFE RIGHT NOW, IN JESUS' MIGHTY NAME.

3. (3) YOU PERSONALITY LIMITING HIS BODY WITH ANY FORM OF AFFLICTION AND INFIRMITY, YOUR TIME IS UP NOW, BY FIRE AND THUNDER IN JESUS' NAME.

4. Matthew 15:13 "Jesus replied, 'Every plant that my heavenly Father has not planted will be pulled up by the roots.'" YOU STRANGE ALTARS STRENGTHENING AFFLICTION AND VOCAL IMPEDIMENT OVER THE LIFE OF OUR SON, EXPIRE NOW, IN THE MIGHTY NAME OF JESUS.

5. Jeremiah 30:17 'But I will restore you to health and heal your wounds,' declares the LORD, 'because you are called an outcast, Zion for whom no one cares.'" LORD! RESTORE AND RENEW THE HEALTH OF ANYONE IN THE FAMILY FROM THE HANDS OF THE DEVIL, IN JESUS' NAME! Matthew 7:7-8 "Keep on asking, and you will receive what you ask for. Keep on seeking, and you will find. Keep on knocking, and the door will be opened to you. For everyone who asks, receives. Everyone who seeks, finds. And to everyone who knocks, the door will be opened."

I kept repeating this over and over during the course of the day, reminding myself of GOD's promises, and HE has been so faithful to us. Now, some of us might be wondering why we need to even pray when GOD sees and feels all our worries, burdens, and suffering, and the truth is, according to Nicky:

God wants us to be a part of the process. Here's how it works. God puts a burden on your heart. It may be for the salvation of someone, or it may be for some other thing.

But when God puts a burden on your heart, you pray. And then you see God do the so-called impossible and answer that prayer.

AMEN! No matter how long it takes for GOD to answer my prayers regarding Jayson, I will keep on praying that HIS will be done. Nicky reminds us that:

If the answer is 'yes' He may be increasing your faith. If the answer is 'wait' He may be increasing your patience. If the answer if 'no' He may have something better in mind.

But ultimately remember that "God's will for you, is good and pleasing and perfect" (Romans 12:2). Therefore, I will continue to be patient and wait on the Lord! Moreover, Nicky reminds us to:

Trust in God's promises and wait patiently, Abraham waited for 25 years. Joseph waited 13 years. Moses waited 25 years. Jesus waited 30 years. If God makes you wait, you are in good company.

AMEN!

M.J. Wotany

Notes

Why persistence in praying to our Heavenly Father pays off!

"Keep on asking, and you will receive what you ask for. Keep on seeking, and you will find. Keep on knocking, and the door will be opened to you. For everyone who asks, receives. Everyone who seeks, finds. And to everyone who knocks, the door will be opened."

—Matthew 7:7-8

If we remember, as children when we wanted to get our way or get something from our parents, we would ask and ask and ask until we become a thorn in our parents' flesh. As we ponder this, our own kids are doing the same things to us right now when they want something. For example, Emmanuella will ask me over and over again to get her these L.O.L. surprise dolls that kids are into now, and my oldest son would beg me constantly for an iPhone until he eventually got one. From these examples, persistence eventually got them what they wanted.

When we go to our Father constantly, frequently, every day, tugging at the hem of HIS garment, HE will answer us. Jesus taught us many, many great lessons through parables; however, for some lessons, one has to truly put their ears down and listen in order to understand, and others may need to meditate on it several times. The parable of persistence in prayers was also explained in further detail when HIS Son showed us why it's important; therefore, we must take it seriously and hold tightly to it daily, for one day GOD will answer us!

Parable of a persistent widow—Luke 18:1-8

One day, Jesus told his disciples a story to show that they should always pray and never give up. "There was a judge in a certain city," he said, "who neither feared God nor cared about people. A widow of that city came to him repeatedly, saying, 'Give me justice in this dispute with my enemy.' The judge ignored her for a while, but finally he said to himself, 'I don't fear God or care about people, but this woman is driving me crazy. I'm going to see that she gets justice, because she is wearing me out with her constant requests!'" Then the Lord said, "Learn a lesson from this unjust judge. Even he rendered a just decision in the end. So don't you think God will surely give justice to his chosen people who cry out to him day and night? Will he keep putting them off? I tell you, he will grant justice to them quickly! But when the Son of Man returns, how many will he find on the earth who have faith?"

Another story of persistence can be found in Luke 11:5-13:

Then, teaching them more about prayer, he used this story: "Suppose you went to a friend's house at midnight, wanting to borrow three loaves of bread. You say to him, 'A friend of mine has just arrived for a visit, and I have nothing for him to eat.' And suppose he calls out from his bedroom, 'Don't bother me. The door is locked for the night, and my family and I are all in bed. I can't help you.' But I tell you this—though he won't do it for friendship's sake, if you keep knocking long enough, he will get up and give you whatever you need because of your shameless persistence. And so I tell you, keep on asking, and you will receive what you ask for. Keep on seeking, and you will find. Keep on knocking, and the door will be opened to you. For everyone who asks, receives. Everyone who seeks, finds. And to everyone who knocks, the door will be opened. You fathers—if your children ask for a fish, do you give them a snake instead? Or if they ask for an egg, do you give them a scorpion? Of course not! So if you sinful people know how to give good gifts to your children, how much more will your heavenly Father give the Holy Spirit to those who ask him."

My dear companions, I know it isn't easy, but we must try to stay connected to GOD in prayer, to be encouraged, and remember to always keep up the faith and that will in turn help us to stay in line with GOD's will!

Below are a few of my favorite Psalms, and I hope they help you stay encouraged and continually abide in HIM!

Psalm 91

¹ Those who live in the shelter of the Most High
   will find rest in the shadow of the Almighty.
² This I declare about the Lord:
He alone is my refuge, my place of safety;
   he is my God, and I trust him.
³ For he will rescue you from every trap
   and protect you from deadly disease.
⁴ He will cover you with his feathers.
   He will shelter you with his wings.
   His faithful promises are your armor and protection.
⁵ Do not be afraid of the terrors of the night,
   nor the arrow that flies in the day.
⁶ Do not dread the disease that stalks in darkness,
   nor the disaster that strikes at midday.
⁷ Though a thousand fall at your side,

though ten thousand are dying around you,
  these evils will not touch you.
[8] Just open your eyes,
  and see how the wicked are punished.
[9] If you make the Lord your refuge,
  if you make the Most High your shelter,
[10] no evil will conquer you;
  no plague will come near your home.
[11] For he will order his angels
  to protect you wherever you go.
[12] They will hold you up with their hands
  so you won't even hurt your foot on a stone.
[13] You will trample upon lions and cobras;
  you will crush fierce lions and serpents under your feet!
[14] The Lord says, "I will rescue those who love me.
  I will protect those who trust in my name.
[15] When they call on me, I will answer;
  I will be with them in trouble.
  I will rescue and honor them.
[16] I will reward them with a long life
  and give them my salvation."

Psalm 136

[1] Give thanks to the Lord, for he is good!
His faithful love endures forever.
[2] Give thanks to the God of gods.
His faithful love endures forever.
[3] Give thanks to the Lord of lords.
His faithful love endures forever.
[4] Give thanks to him who alone does mighty miracles.
His faithful love endures forever.
[5] Give thanks to him who made the heavens so skillfully.

His faithful love endures forever.
⁶ Give thanks to him who placed the earth among the waters.
His faithful love endures forever.
⁷ Give thanks to him who made the heavenly lights—
His faithful love endures forever.
⁸ the sun to rule the day,
His faithful love endures forever.
⁹ and the moon and stars to rule the night.
His faithful love endures forever.
¹⁰ Give thanks to him who killed the firstborn of Egypt.
His faithful love endures forever.
¹¹ He brought Israel out of Egypt.
His faithful love endures forever.
¹² He acted with a strong hand and powerful arm.
His faithful love endures forever.
¹³ Give thanks to him who parted the Red Sea.[a]
His faithful love endures forever.
¹⁴ He led Israel safely through,
His faithful love endures forever.
¹⁵ but he hurled Pharaoh and his army into the Red Sea.
His faithful love endures forever.
¹⁶ Give thanks to him who led his people through the
     wilderness.
His faithful love endures forever.
¹⁷ Give thanks to him who struck down mighty kings.
His faithful love endures forever.
¹⁸ He killed powerful kings—
His faithful love endures forever.
¹⁹ Sihon king of the Amorites,
His faithful love endures forever.
²⁰ and Og king of Bashan.
His faithful love endures forever.
²¹ God gave the land of these kings as an inheritance—

His faithful love endures forever.
[22] a special possession to his servant Israel.
His faithful love endures forever.
[23] He remembered us in our weakness.
His faithful love endures forever.
[24] He saved us from our enemies.
His faithful love endures forever.
[25] He gives food to every living thing.
His faithful love endures forever.
[26] Give thanks to the God of heaven.
His faithful love endures forever.

Notes

Lastly When You Feel Like Giving Up, P.U.S.H!

Pray Until Something Happens

"*I tell you the truth, you can say to this mountain, 'May you be lifted up and thrown into the sea', and it will happen. But you must really believe it will happen and have no doubt in your heart.*"

—Mark 11:23

Is it okay to discipline even with the diagnosis?

"Those who spare the rod of discipline hate their children. Those who love their children care enough to discipline them."

—*Proverbs 13:24*

S INCE ALL OF us come from different homes and embrace discipline differently, it is sometimes hard for two people to come together and make children and try to agree on how to raise these children. The one thing is that, though I was born in Africa, I have spent almost the last thirty years of my life in America; therefore, choosing a partner for me was very difficult. I battled with this for a really long time and ended up marrying an African from the same tribe as my family. Our beliefs, thoughts, processes, and ways of doing things should have been similar, but they weren't. Though on the cultural aspect we understood each other more, the ways we would discipline our children I knew would be different.

Don't get me wrong, I am truly blessed with the partner I married, though we have had our own ups and downs (but which marriage doesn't?). Though this situation with Jayson could easily have separated us, I thank GOD for giving us the patience to endure it all. In James 1:2-4, the Bible states: "Dear brothers and sisters, when troubles of any kind come your way, consider it an opportunity for great joy. For you know that when your faith is tested, your endurance has a chance to grow. So let it grow, for when your endurance is fully developed, you will be perfect and complete, needing nothing." That's where I wanted to be . . . .needing absolutely NOTHING! Furthermore, as it has been said, "Every storm is a school. Every trial is a test. Every experience is an education. Every difficulty is for your development." (Referenced in Gumbel, 2018).

My husband had his own challenges, and I also had mine, and it was kind of hard for us to come to the middle to realize how we could be better parents. I think honestly that we parents learn every day about how to continue to become better and better parents. Here we are with a few marital difficulties, Jayson, and our other two kids. We were trying to make sense of everything, and it wasn't an easy journey.

A little additional background about myself—in 2008, I was looking for a part-time job to work along with my full-time one, and a friend of mine introduced me to respite services through Catholic Charities. I started in November 2008 working with kids with behavioral difficulties, ranging in age from four to eighteen. Fast forward to 2018, I've now been in this field for ten years. I would never have imagined that the skills I use in my part-time job would be the same skills I needed for my own child. I tried the best I could to treat my own child, not as a client, but as my own flesh and blood. I utilized the skills I use with my clients in order to better cope with Jayson's challenges at home. Though this was a challenge in my own home, I never knew that the Lord was preparing to use me and the skills I learned over the years. This allowed me to have the patience to deal with Jayson daily, especially on the behavioral aspect, and this was when and where my husband and I would disagree the most.

I understood that Jayson needed to be disciplined, because growing up we had to be disciplined severely since our father was a teacher. He didn't take any nonsense, and our mom was our comforter. However, I knew that I couldn't treat Jayson the same way I treated Emma or Carlson. Furthermore, I knew that "to discipline a child produces wisdom, but a mother is disgraced by an undisciplined child" (Proverbs 29:15). Jayson didn't understand when you said, "sit and be quiet," or "you are in time out," or "stop jumping," or "stop hurting yourself by hitting your forehead on the wall or on the wood of the couch." He never understood his limits or what was wrong or right. He didn't understand what could hurt him and what couldn't or that punishment meant he did something wrong.

Since I was Jayson's comforter, whenever his dad would discipline him, I would comfort him and try, the key word here is *try*, to make him understand that he couldn't keep doing the things he was doing. One of the main things that really irritated my husband was the fact that Jayson couldn't control his bouncing, even after purchasing the trampoline, and the couch was still his go-to place to bounce. I understood where my husband was coming from because the couch set did cost us a lot of money, but I also knew that Jayson wasn't doing it on purpose to get disciplined—he just didn't know any better.

Another behavioral difficulty that Jayson experienced was not being aware of his surroundings and always wanting to throw anything and everything, anywhere. One day, he was in the living room watching TV and got mad about something and threw one of his toys behind his back and accidentally cracked the screen of our 65-inch TV. Both the TV and couches being messed up, my husband thought that Jayson knew what he was doing and just didn't want to stop. How does a mother respect her husband and still protect her child from being disciplined when they are not aware of what is happening? This is what I mean about struggling to determine where the line starts or stops when it comes to disciplining our kiddos, and this struggle is real, my companions, especially in African households. So I had to try to find ways to protect Jayson from being disciplined for things that were hard for him to control or understand and also to balance my relationship with my husband in order for us to not keep arguing or having so many ups and downs.

Well, for us, I appreciate all that my husband did to try to keep Jayson in line because it paid off, though our marriage went through a lot. If it hadn't been for the things my husband did, I think Jayson would be even more out of control than he is today. Discipline is necessary, not only for sanity in the household, but also for appropriate behavior out in public, as I described in the Chipotle incident earlier. It was only after that incident and others that occurred in the home that I realized that some sort of discipline HAS to take place for him to know that a line has to be drawn and that there are rules in place to follow. Even now, though Jayson continues to struggle with jumping on the couches, at least when we yell once, he calms down and knows his place and quickly adjusts. What helped us even more when it came to discipline was:

1. This was the best advice another prophet gave me— for us to read the children's Bible to Jayson daily. This not only helped him to absorb the Word but also helped in breaking those chains that bind his tongue and keeping the devil away when it came to Jayson achieving his purpose and destiny for his life. In reading GOD's Word, we realized that the book of Proverbs repeatedly tells us the importance and

reasons why we have to discipline our children, and these were why we thought discipline was important, even with a diagnosis of autism:

- *"You will say, 'How I hated discipline! If only I had not ignored all the warnings!'" (Proverbs 5:12)*

- *"To learn, you must love discipline; it is stupid to hate correction." (Proverbs 12:1)*

- *"A wise child accepts a parent's discipline; a mocker refuses to listen to correction." (Proverbs 13:1)*

- *"Only a fool despises a parent's discipline; whoever learns from correction is wise." (Proverbs 15:5)*

- *"Discipline your children while there is hope. Otherwise you will ruin their lives." (Proverbs 19:18)*

- *"A youngster's heart is filled with foolishness but physical discipline will drive it far away." (Proverbs 22:15)*

- *"Don't fail to discipline your children. The rod of punishment won't kill them." (Proverbs 23:23)*

2. Positive reinforcement when not jumping on the couch and actually using his trampoline

3. Empowering him to get involved in activities at home, such as cleaning or taking things from upstairs to Dad or downstairs to Grandmother, etc.

4. We were also very repetitive, extremely repetitive!

5. Making an effort to take him out to other homes in order for him to interact with his peers and him being active in our Thursday Night Alive Bible study group

All of this drastically helped in controlling Jayson's behaviors and in disciplining him a lot better in the home and out in the community.

Nonetheless, this is a topic that I believe is every parent's duty to try to see if they can make an impact in their child's behavior by taking small steps to address their behavioral difficulties. At times, as parents, though we feel bad that our kiddos don't really understand what's happening, there is a small part of them that I truly believe wants to act right. They want to listen and not be disruptive. They don't want to be in trouble. They want to be held accountable for their behavior. Trust me, one day they will thank us for not giving up on them!

When it comes to discipline, each of us have our own approach and opinion as well. However, for Jayson, timeout just didn't work (as I mentioned earlier). More importantly, what might work for our family might not work for yours; however, I believe every kiddo needs to know and understand boundaries. Every kid needs to know that every behavior has a consequence, and the earlier they know this, the quicker they can embrace being disciplined. Being aware of that, we used our foreign straightforwardness and sternness that our parents used on us. We thought, if we turned out fine, obviously our parents did something right. In addition, with Jayson we not only had be to be extremely repetitive, we had to visually show him how to change his behavior from what he was doing wrong to what he had to do that was correct. We continue to do this, to reassure and praise him when he does things the right way.

"Fathers, do not provoke your children to anger by the way you treat them. Rather, bring them up with the discipline and instruction that comes from the Lord."

—*Ephesians 6:4*

Notes

Sibling's perspective

"Children are a gift from the Lord; they are a reward from him."

—*Psalms 127:3*

Emmanuella and Jayson 9/21/2014

Emmanuella and Jayson December 2018

So, a little bit more history about our family. Jayson is the last of three. He has an older brother who is eighteen and a sister who is six. The eighteen-year-old didn't grow up with us. He came to the United States when he was fifteen. When he arrived, I felt like I quickly needed to explain to him what was going on with his sibling. I sat him down and explained to him that Jayson has a hard time expressing himself like other kids his age, so he receives additional services to help him with this. Because in Africa we don't have terms such as *autism* or *developmental delay*, I had to let him know the easiest way I could that his sibling couldn't talk and because of having this difficulty, he at times gets frustrated at trying to tell anyone something. It also just happened that around the time he was arriving, Jayson was scheduled to have his hearing test done for the doctors to rule out any hearing deficits, and my stepson accompanied us to the appointment. Naturally, he understood what was going on and easily adapted.

Emmanuella, the six-year-old sister, on the other hand, had the hardest time. Since Jayson was getting the special educator, the occupational therapist, a psychiatrist, and later the ABA technicians, there were a lot of people in and out of our home. Emma kept wondering why she wasn't getting anyone to come see her and play with her, not knowing or understanding what Jayson was going through. This really had an impact on Emma and became another challenge for me. I was so thankful that my stepson didn't really need me. However, how could I split myself in half between Emma and Jayson? How could I show the younger kids that I love them equally, though one needs me more than the other? I knew Emma needed me, but in a different way. She kept saying that I loved Jayson more than her and that Jayson is a better child than her and that's why he gets all of mommy's attention. I had to do something drastic and had to do it quickly.

1. I sat Emma down and explained to her that Jayson has a different way of learning, and he needs more people to teach him. I told her that I wanted her to be his number one teacher....Oh my goodness,

did she take this literally (you will see what I mean later).

2. I got my family members involved in helping me make time for Emma to take her out, spend time with her, and make her not miss me. Emma was gone almost every weekend with her aunt to play with others, go shopping, or just have her own one-on-one time, which was the best blessing I could've asked for!

3. I got Emma involved in Jayson's activities. For example, because Jayson was so sensory seeking, an OT suggested that I make a sensory bowl at home. I made one of all types of beans, spoons, cups, squishy things, etc., and added letters and numbers since at the time Emma and I were working on alphabet recognition. Incorporating Emma in our sensory bowl was the best thing I ever did! Look at our bowl . . . Isn't it beautiful?!

4. During Jayson's ABA sessions, it was Emma and Mom's sessions. We would watch movies or do our nails and just have that time together that Emma desperately craved. And lastly,

5. I encouraged Emma to talk, teach, and reinforce to Jayson what she learned in school, at home. Emma took this and ran with it. She would reinforce body parts, colors, and numbers—anything she should think of. She felt so empowered, and this influenced the way she started to "see" Jayson's need to have people come see him for services. My job was finally done!

My companions, that's the power of empowerment. Empowering even children to do things changes one's perspective and changes their view on whatever challenge they might be having. I praise GOD for giving me the wisdom and knowledge on how to handle this difficulty in the midst of Jayson's own difficulty and me not losing Emma's love for me or her love for her brother. The part that I was most blessed with was the fact that during those moments that I couldn't figure out what Emma wanted, I would buy her things just to shut her up. Thankfully, Jayson never got angry because he never understood what was going on; moreover, he couldn't talk to me and tell me even if he was mad at me for buying Emma things. This truly showed me that ". . . we know that GOD causes everything to work together for good of those who love God (HIM) and are called according to his purpose for them" (Romans 8:28). Jayson went with the flow and I was truly thankful for that. And now, every time Jayson imitates/repeats anything Emma does or says, she is quick to high five him, and quickly finds me, Dad, brother, or grandparents to tell us what Jayson did or said! #Jaysonsnumber1cheerleader!

"Direct your children onto the right path, and when they are older, they will not leave it."

—*Proverbs 22:6*

Notes

Jayson . . . NOW

"The Lord is my strength and shield. I trust Him with all my heart. He helps me, and my heart is filled with joy. I burst out in songs of thanksgiving."

—Psalms 28:7

M Y DEAR COMPANIONS, as our journey comes to a pause, not an end, because it will continue, I want to give you an update regarding how far Jayson has come. I am doing this to let you all know that we truly serve a Mighty GOD who can do whatever He wants, whenever HE wants. He has taken Jayson through this journey, and I give HIM all the praise for keeping me still and sane in the midst of it all. Though I came to terms in accepting that my child has autism, my relationship with GOD grew even closer because of it. I don't think I would have drawn myself closer to GOD if I hadn't gone through this test, trial, tribulation, rough patch, difficulty, crisis, sadness, etc. Through this battle I started to read HIS Word more, I started to teach the Bible to our Thursday night Alive children at our church, I started to encourage other parents about the power of healing through Jesus Christ, and finally, I thought to share this experience with you all.

Right now, Jayson is making so much progress that his teachers, speech pathologists, and ABA technicians from last year see the growth he has made from then until now, all to the Glory of GOD! Even our pastor notices that Jayson is able to sit and pay attention during our circle time at Bible study.

In December 2018, I thought to myself and later on mentioned to his Speech Language Pathologist who does Prompting with him that I wanted to work on his potty-training during winter break. I told myself that I'd be off work and the kids would be home anyway—why not depend on GOD to get us through those two weeks since ABA had been working on it for so long? My dear companions, when you have FAITH and a GOD who has your back, nothing can stop you! By the end of the two weeks, GOD had Jayson going to the bathroom in the toilet— not only peeing, but also pooping. Have any of you all ever heard such a thing? It took less than two weeks and Jayson was fully trained—now if that isn't GOD, I don't know who it is, because it wasn't me! I gave HIM the glory that week, and from then on, Jayson has been going on the bus to school, to church, and everywhere with no diaper on. The nighttime training will come another time . . . no worries! It's amazing what GOD can do when you have faith and you "never stop praying" (1 Thessalonians 5:17). If HE can do that for me, He can also do that for you, if you hold tightly to HIS Word, stay encouraged, have faith, know this now and always that the Lord reigns over every area of your life and wants to bring restoration to it.

I also truly thank GOD for the people He placed in Jayson's life who have been with him during this journey. It truly takes a village to raise a child, and I am so thankful for Jayson's team from Willoughby Beach Pediatrics, Smiles4Children, Kennedy Krieger Institute, Humanum, Featherbed Lane Elementary, Connec-to-Talk, and last but not least, Hunting Ridge Presbyterian Church. There are two speech pathologist who pushed Jayson and treated him like he was human. My dear companions, you know what I mean when I say this. There are moments when people either in the medical or mental health fields lose their sense of humanity and are quick to want to label or diagnose our children for one reason or another. But there was this one speech pathologist in the Achievements program who pushed Jayson to his limits over the summer of 2018. Within three months, she had transitioned him from using the Go-Talk to using an iPad Touch Chat Device, which has been tremendously helpful for him. It fills in the gaps when he is having difficulty communicating. With her thoroughness in the report, by the time he was starting school in September 2018, the Assistive Technology device team for Baltimore County Public Schools didn't need to re-evaluate him again and he quickly got his own device to start using at school and home during his ABA sessions.

The other speech pathologist who has been supportive is the one who helps Jayson with the Prompting program. This lady was so bubbly from the first day we met and continues to bring that vibrant energy with her every time she meets with Jayson. She was so encouraging and really came down to my level. I thanked her for her honesty because she told me that the other speech pathologist who Jayson sees was quickly trying to diagnose him with Apraxia. Apraxia, according to the National Institutes of Health, is a "neurological disorder that affects the brain pathways involved in planning the sequence of movements involved in producing speech. The brain knows what it wants to say, but cannot properly plan and sequence the required speech sound movements." She, however, thought it was more of a speech delay, which is why earlier I mentioned all about the importance of who you allow to be in the presence of your child to help them through this.

Last but not least, we are thankful for the ABA technician we had through Humanim who has stuck with us even after their ABA program shut down. The company could no longer maintain its staff or provide the hours that Jayson was approved for in the home. On the last visit, she told us that once we found a company that would provide services for Jayson, we should let her know and she would continue seeing him alongside her full-time job . . . now that is a BLESSING! So after a few calls, we found another company and I quickly told her. She applied, went for the interview, and was hired. GOD IS SO FAITHFUL! So now, we still have our original ABA technician from when we started, and Jayson is her only client. If not GOD, who else? So truly like Romans 8:28 tells us "and we know that God causes everything to work together for the good of those who love God and are called according to his purpose for them."

Below is Jayson's schedule for November 2018, and he is going strong; ALL to the GLORY OF GOD! THANK YOU ABBA, FATHER!

SUN	MON	TUE	WED	THU	FRI	SAT
				01 **Achievements** 9:30-11:30am, **School** 1:10-3:50 pm **ABA** 4:30-7:30 pm	**02** **Achievements** 9:30-11:30am, **School** 1:10-3:50 pm **ABA** 5:30-7:30	**03**
04	**05** Achievements 9:30-11:30am, **Prompting** 11:30-12 pm **School** 1:10-3:50pm **ABA** 5:30-7:30 pm	**06** **Achievements** 9:30-11:30am, **School** 1:10-3:50 pm **ABA** 4:30-7:30 pm	**07** **Achievements** 9:30-11:30am, **School** 1:10-3:50 pm **ABA** 5:30-7:30	**08** **Achievements** 9:30-11:30am, **School** 1:10-3:50 pm **ABA** 4:30-7:30 pm	**09** **Achievements** 9:30-11:30am, **School** 1:10-3:50 pm **ABA** 5:30-7:30	**10**
11	**12** Achievements 9:30-11:30am, **Prompting** 11:30-12 pm **School** 1:10-3:50pm **ABA** 5:30-7:30 pm	**13** **Achievements** 9:30-11:30am, **School** 1:10-3:50pm **ABA** 4:30-7:30 pm	**14** **Achievements** 9:30-11:30am, **School** 1:10-3:50pm **ABA** 5:30-7:30	**15** **Achievements** 9:30-11:30am, **School** 1:10-3:50 pm **ABA** 4:30-7:30 pm	**16** **Achievements** 9:30-11:30am, **School** 1:10-3:50 pm **ABA** 5:30-7:30	**17**

18	19	20	21	22	23	24
	Achievements 9:30-11:30am, **Prompting** 11:30-12pm **School** 1:10-3:50pm **ABA** 5:30-7:30 pm	**Achievements** 9:30-11:30am, **School** 1:10-3:50 pm **ABA** 4:30-7:30 pm	**Achievements** 9:30-11:30am, **School** 1:10-3:50 **ABA** 5:30-7:30	HOLIDAY	HOLIDAY	

25	26	27	28	29	30
	Achievements 9:30-11:30am, **Prompting** 11:30-12 pm **School** 1:10-3:50 pm **ABA** 5:30-7:30 pm	**Achievements** 9:30-11:30am, **School** 1:10-3:50 pm **ABA** 4:30-7:30 pm	**Achievements** 9:30-11:30am, **School** 1:10-3:50 pm **ABA** 5:30-7:30	**Achievements** 9:30-11:30am, **School** 1:10-3:50 pm **ABA** 4:30-7:30 pm	**Achievements** 9:30-11:30am, **School** 1:10-3:50 pm **ABA** 5:30-7:30

"All of this is for your benefit. And as God's grace reaches more and more people, there will be great thanksgiving, and God will receive more and more glory."

—2 Corinthians 4:15

Notes

Final Thought

"But when you ask him, be sure that your faith is in God alone. Do not waver, for a person with divided loyalty is as unsettled as a wave of the sea that is blown and tossed by the wind. Such people should not expect to receive anything from the Lord. Their loyalty is divided between God and the world, and they are unstable in everything they do."

—James 1:6-8

MY DEAR COMPANIONS, as this part of Jayson's journey with you comes to a pause, I truly hope you have learned one or two things from us. One of the main takeaways from all of this is, as Nicky states, "In this life, there will always be trials and testing. It is never going to be without times of turmoil. However, the moment that you believe the gospel, you have the promise of God's eventual and eternal rest." AMEN!

I hope I gave you some insight on what worked for us during this experience and what didn't. Ultimately, I hope you can pass this down to others to also be inspired and informed so that we can help each other. More importantly, like Nicky states:

Stand firm together as a strong community. You are not on your own. God never intended you to fight your battles alone. He called you to be a part of a strong, healthy, vibrant, growing community of his people. Together you can stand firm, not only resisting backsliding but moving forward.

Together as a community, we can accomplish so much more than we ever could as individuals. As we share information with each other, the more we bless, uplift, and love each other as God taught and told us to.

In conclusion, as we share this information with each other and grow in faith, Nicky tells us, "Your key to getting your life sorted out is Jesus. Your key to understanding the Bible is Jesus. Your key to understanding God's character is Jesus. Your key to life is Jesus." My companions, our KEY to the healing of our kiddos is JESUS! We must go to HIM to get to the Father and ask for anything and it shall be given to us. Let us remember that our GOD is NOT a man and that His Word teaches us in Luke 21:33 that "Heaven and earth shall pass away: but my [HIS] words shall not pass away." You ask why? Because HE is the PROMISE KEEPER!

AS WE WAIT PATIENTLY FOR JESUS' RETURN, LET'S STAND FIRM ON HIS WORD!

Prayer: Lord, I thank you for this opportunity you have given me to share Jayson's testimony with others. Father, we give you all the glory and praise for who you are in our lives and what you continue to do. Jehovah, we come before you, asking that you forgive us for all our sins, those knowingly and unknowingly. Lord, we repent of our sins and ask that you cleanse us from all unrighteousness. Heavenly Father, we pray that you come into our midst today as we need your healing and restoration for our children. Lord, we ask that you

loose those chains that the enemy has put upon our children, and may each of them achieve their GOD-given purpose in life today by the power of the Holy Spirit. Lord, we ask that this testimony may touch the lives of so many people, here in the United States and around the world, and all the glory be given to YOU and YOU ALONE! May YOUR WILL be done in lives today, tomorrow, and for the rest of our lives. We ask this through CHRIST our LORD! AMEN, AMEN, and AMEN!

"I also tell you this: If two of you agree here on earth concerning anything you ask, my Father in heaven will do it for you."

—Matthew 18:19

"For all of God's promises have been fulfilled in Christ with a resounding 'Yes!' And through Christ, our 'Amen' (which means 'Yes') ascends to God for his Glory."

—2 Corinthians 1:20

Notes

Venues that Accommodate Children with Autism

"Yet it was our weaknesses he carried; it was our sorrows that weighed him down. And we thought his troubles were a punishment from God, a punishment for his own sins! But he was pierced for our rebellion, crushed for our sins. He was beaten so we could be whole. He was whipped so we could be healed."

—*Isaiah 53:4-5*

My companions, as there continues to be more awareness regarding this diagnosis, more organizations are doing what they can to lessen the burdens on us parents when it comes to activities, shopping, or even time during the holidays. Also, please check out your local malls for sensory times, for pictures with Santa, Easter bunnies, or Halloween and other events that allow extra time that our kiddos need. I hope you find this information useful.

1. Imagination Stage

Sensory Friendly Performances

From their website: "Each production within our Lerner Family Theatre Season features a Sensory-Friendly performance designed to be more accessible for those individuals on the autism spectrum and their families.

Our Sensory-Friendly performances aim to provide a safe and welcoming environment where families can simply relax and be who they are. Tickets to Sensory-Friendly Performances are $12-$25 and 100% refundable up until the show begins." "ADAPTATIONS FOR A SENSORY-FRIENDLY PERFORMANCE A pre-visit social story, video, and other preparatory materials for parents and children explaining what to expect Glow sticks raised when a surprise will happen on stage Reduction of the sound level and bright stage lighting Low lighting in the theatre so patrons can easily move around or exit the theatre Limited crowds and "seating holes" to allow space between families Designated spaces for those who need a quieter area to take a break Allowance for the use of tablets and smartphones for communication" ***Please check Buddy's Maryland Recreation blog post for details on Imagination Stage's accessible performing arts classes.

4908 Auburn Avenue
Bethesda, MD 20814
301-280-1660

2. Port Discovery

Discovery Weeks and Discovery Days

From the museum: "Port Discovery welcomes guests of all abilities to experience our Museum, interactive exhibits and learning through play. A variety of services and programs are available for individuals and children with disabilities and special needs."

35 Market Place
Baltimore, MD 21202
410-864-2664

3. The Walters Art Museum

Your entire family is cordially invited to a Sensory Morning at the Walters Art Museum. Join us for a morning of accessible museum programming designed specifically for children with Sensory Processing Disorders and their entire family. Educators from the Walters Art Museum and therapists from

Kennedy Krieger Institute will be present for the entirety of the event.

We are here to help your family have a great time! Accommodations will be made in consideration of unique sensory needs. Visual resources, tactile activities, sensory breaks, hand fidgets, and opportunities for guidance and structured support will be available throughout the galleries. Meet professionals and advocates from community organizations at our sensory-friendly resource fair!

We welcome

- Kids being kids!
- Children's voices
- Weighted blankets and weighted vests
- Earplugs and headphones
- Hand fidgets
- Sensory breaks
- Wheelchairs and other mobility devices

Schedule

- 9–11 a.m. Art activity in a private studio, with adjoining space for sensory breaks
- 9–11 a.m. Facilitated activities in the Arts of Asia galleries
- 10 a.m. Doors open to the public; activities continue

600 N. Charles Street
Baltimore, MD 21201
410-547-9000, ext. 300

National Chains That May Have Sensory-Friendly Activities in Your Area:

We Rock the Spectrum Kid's Gym

The Gym for All Kids

From their website: "We Rock the Spectrum Kids Gyms was founded to provide a place for children of all ability levels to play and grow together. As the only kids gym that offers an inclusive philosophy we have found all children can benefit from our uniquely designed sensory equipment that is specifically designed to aid children with sensory processing disorders. However, in our experience, all children are able to benefit greatly from this equipment and by allowing children of all ability levels to play together they are able to learn a great deal from each other and become the best motivation for success on every level.

Our Gym Includes:

- Suspended equipment with swings – for balance and vestibular treatment
- Crash mats and crash pillows – for fun, motor planning, and strength
- Zip line – for stress release and joint and body relaxation
- Trampoline – for building leg and core strength
- Indoor play structure – for climbing and increasing playground skills
- Sensory-based toys – for improved auditory processing and fine motor skills
- Fine Motor and Arts and Crafts Area – for improved hand-eye coordination"

Autism Eats

Autism Friendly Dining

http://www.autismeats.org/events.html

From their webpage: Providing autism-friendly non-judgmental environments for family dining, socializing and connecting with others who share similar joys and challenges. ALL behaviors are welcomed!

Check the website for restaurants and dates!

Cobb Theatres

Sensory Friendly Films

Sensory Friendly showings provide families with varying abilities the opportunity to enjoy a family friendly film where kids can be kids in a safe and accepting environment. The auditoriums are made comfortable by brighter lights and the sound level is turned down. The audience is encouraged to be themselves and interact with the movie, while having fun without the worry of disturbing others. Dance, sing and enjoy the show!!!

All shows will begin at 10am local time. Films, dates and program are subject to change. Tickets are available in person only the Wednesday prior to each showing.

Marcus Theaters

REEL MOVIES FOR Real Needs

A Special Showing for Families and Individuals with Special Needs. We understand that sometimes it is difficult or uncomfortable for families with special needs children to attend movies together.

Marcus Theatres Reel Movies for Reel Needs is a specially designed program to serve families with special needs such as autism or other challenges, who seldom attend movies. Reel Movies for Real Needs creates a welcoming and comfortable environment – lower sound, lights up – where families with children who need accommodations will be able to share the experience of seeing family friendly films at a theatre.

Urban Air Adventure Park

Sensory Friendly Screenings

- A pillar of SMG's Outreach since 2003, our monthly Special Needs Screenings are designed for families raising children with special needs. Special Needs Screenings are shown with the lights up and the volume lowered and children are free to move around, talk, or even dance in the aisles during the movie.

- The sensory friendly screenings are free for children with special needs and their siblings. Adult tickets are available at before-noon price. There are no advance ticket sales. Parental guidance is always suggested.

- Special Needs Screenings are shown at 11:00 am at all SMG locations except EpiCentre. SMG Downey, Monrovia and Redlands look forward to offering our special needs screening program in the near future. We are currently in process of installing new seating and will subsequently undergo remodeling to our full concept. These locations will offer special needs screenings as soon as this work has been completed.

Studio Movie Grill

Sensory Friendly Screenings

A pillar of SMG's Outreach since 2003, our monthly Special Needs Screenings are designed for families raising children with special needs. Special Needs Screenings are shown with the lights up and the volume lowered and children are free to move around, talk, or even dance in the aisles during the movie.

The sensory friendly screenings are free for children with special needs and their siblings. Adult tickets are available at before-noon price. There are no advance ticket sales. Parental guidance is always suggested.

Special Needs Screenings are shown at 11:00 am at all SMG locations except EpiCentre. SMG Downey, Monrovia and Redlands look forward to offering our special needs screening program in the near future. We are currently in process of installing new seating and will subsequently undergo remodeling to our full concept. These locations will offer special needs screenings as soon as this work has been completed.

Regal Cinemas

My Way Matinee

Sensory friendly movie screenings with sounds lower, lights brighter.

AMC Theaters

Sensory Friendly Films

AMC is proud to partner with the Autism Society to offer unique movie showings where we turn the lights up, and turn the sound down, so you can get up, dance, walk, shout or sing! Our Sensory Friendly Film program is available on the second and fourth Saturday (family-friendly) and Tuesday evenings (mature audiences) of every month. Please check your local theatre listings for specific showtimes, and don't forget to share your family fun with #AMCSensoryFriendly.

Major Airports

Wings for Autism®/Wings for All®

- Wings for Autism®/Wings for All® are airport "rehearsals" specially designed for individuals with autism spectrum disorders and individuals with intellectual/developmental disabilities. The programs are designed to alleviate the stress that families who have a child with autism or intellectual/developmental disabilities experience when flying. It provides families the opportunity to practice entering the airport, obtaining boarding passes, going through security and boarding a plane. Airport, airline, Transportation Security Administration professionals, and other personnel also have the opportunity to observe, interact, and deliver their services in a structured learning environment.

Sky Zone

Sensory Hours

Enjoy the freedom of jumping. Sensory hours provide a quieter, toned-down jumping experience for those with special needs.

Chuck E. Cheese

Sensory Sensitive Sundays

- Chuck E. Cheese's is proud to support families who have children with autism and special needs. We now offer a sensory-friendly experience on the first Sunday of every month. Our trained and caring staff is there to make sure each guest has a fun filled visit. The Sensory Sensitive Sundays experience includes:
    - ◻ Less crowding and noise
    - ◻ Dimmed lighting
    - ◻ Show and music turned off or down
    - ◻ Limited appearances by Chuck E.
    - ◻ Food and games are offered

iFly

All Abilities Night

All Abilities Night at iFLY is a unique event that makes the dream of flight a reality for those in the special needs community. This program has been custom designed for those with physical and cognitive challenges to create an environment of support and inclusion, while focusing on making what seems impossible, possible.

"Great faith is a product of great fights. Great testimonies are the outcome of great tests. Great triumphs can only come out of great trials."

—*Smith Wigglesworth*

Notes

Recommendations of Autism-Friendly Vacation Destinations—In the U.S. and Around the World

"When I was a child, I spoke and thought and reasoned as a child. But when I grew up, I put away childish things. Now we see things imperfectly, like puzzling reflections in a mirror, but then we will see everything with perfect clarity. All that I know now is partial and incomplete, but then I will know everything completely, just as God now knows me completely."

—*1 Corinthians 13:11-12*

My dear companions, as you all may know, traveling and taking our kiddos on vacation is extremely difficult; however, below are a list of great places that accommodate autistic children. I hope you and your family have fun!

- **Austin, Texas—Austin Nature and Science Center, the Thinkery children's museum, the Austin Aquarium, and swimming at Barton Springs**
- **Beaches Caribbean Resorts**
- **The Berkshires**
- **Camping**
- **Caribbean Cruise**
- **Disney Parks & Resorts**
- **Dollywood**
- **Edaville Family Theme Park**
- **Great America Theme Parks**
- **Great Sand Dunes National Park**
- **Great Wolf Lodge**

- **Greece with A Million Senses**
- **Hershey Park**
- **King's Island Theme Park**
- **LEGOLAND Florida Resort**
- **London, England**
- **Madison, Wisconsin**
- **Morgan's Wonderland**
- **Myrtle Beach, South Carolina**
- **Portugal with 4 All Senses**
- **San Diego Zoo**
- **SeaWorld**
- **Skiing in Colorado**
- **Smuggler's Notch Resort**
- **Snow Mountain Ranch**
- **Surfside Beach, South Carolina**
- **TradeWinds Island Resort**
- **Wilderness Resort**
- **Yellowstone National Park**

"God is the God of promise. Faith involves trusting the promises of God. God makes a promise; faith believes it, hope anticipates it, patience quietly waits for it."

—*Nicky Gumbel*

References

"So God has given both his promise and his oath. These two things are unchangeable because it is impossible for God to lie. Therefore, we who have fled to him for refuge can have great confidence as we hold to the hope that lies before us. This hope is a strong and trustworthy anchor for our souls. It leads us through the curtain into God's inner sanctuary."

—Hebrews 6:18-19

Applied Behavior Analysis Programs Guide—30 Best Autism-Friendly Vacation Ideas
https://www.appliedbehavioranalysisprograms.com/30-best-autism-friendly-vacation-ideas/#chapter1

Belikebuddy.com—sensory friendly activities in MD https://www.belikebuddy.com/maryland

Conley, Bayless Pray Effectively. October 29, 2017 http://www.answersbc.org

Buchan, Angus 21 Days on the Power of Prayer. February 21, 2018. ttp://www.cumbooks.co.za/

Gumbel, Nicky and Pippa, HTB. Bible in One Year 2018. https://www.bibleinoneyear.org/

Shirer, Priscilla. The Armor of God. November 26, 2017. www.lifeway.com

Stephen Neill, *The Supremacy of Jesus*, (Word Publishing, 1984) pg. 47.

U.S. Department of Health and Human Services—Center for Disease Control and Prevention (signs and symptoms—Autism Spectrum Disorder ASD)

https://www.cdc.gov/ncbddd/autism/signs.html

U.S. Department of Health and Human Services—National Institutes of Health—National Institute on Deafness and other Communication Disorder (NIDCD) *Apraxia of Speech* https://www.nidcd.nih.gov/health/apraxia-speech

"Do all the good you can, by all the means you can, in all the ways you can, in all the places you can, at all the times you can, to all the people you can, as long as ever you can."

—*John Wesley*